WE ARE
CALLED

...

TO DO THE
RIGHT THING

WE ARE
CALLED
...
TO DO THE
RIGHT THING

a PRACTICAL GUIDE *for* LEADERS *based*
on PERSONAL REFLECTIONS & EXPERIENCE
from a LONGTIME HIGHER EDUCATION LEADER

by Prakash Mathew

Legacy Series
Volume 1

NDSU | NORTH DAKOTA STATE UNIVERSITY PRESS

Fargo, ND

NDSU | NORTH DAKOTA STATE UNIVERSITY PRESS

NDSU Dept. 2360
P.O. Box 6050
Fargo, ND 58108-6050

We Are Called . . . To Do the Right Thing: A Practical Guide for Leaders Based on Personal Reflections and Experience from a Longtime Higher Education Leader
By Prakash Mathew

Legacy Series Volume 1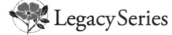

First Edition
First Printing

Library of Congress Control Number: 2021933153
ISBN: 978-1-946163-28-8

The publication of *We Are Called . . . To Do the Right Thing: A Practical Guide for Leaders Based on Personal Reflections and Experience from a Longtime Higher Education Leader* is made possible by the generous support of donors to the NDSU Press Fund and the NDSU Press Endowment Fund, and other contributors to NDSU Press.

Cover design by Jamie Trosen
Interior design by Deb Tanner

David Bertolini, Director
Suzzanne Kelley, Publisher
Zachary Vietz, Publicist, Graduate Assistant in Publishing
Nataly Routledge, Editorial Intern

Printed in Canada

Publisher's Cataloging-In-Publication Data
(Prepared by The Donohue Group, Inc.)

Names: Mathew, Prakash, author.
Title: We are called ... to do the right thing : a practical guide for leaders based on personal reflections and experience from a longtime higher education leader / by Prakash Mathew.
Description: Fargo, ND : North Dakota State University Press, [2021] | Series: Legacy series ; volume 1 | Includes bibliographical references and index.
Identifiers: ISBN 9781946163288
Subjects: LCSH: Educational leadership. | Servant leadership. | Universities and colleges--Administration--Philosophy. | Mathew, Prakash. | College administrators--North Dakota. | BISAC: EDUCATION / Philosophy, Theory & Social Aspects. | EDUCATION / Leadership. | EDUCATION / Higher.
Classification: LCC LB2341 .M38 2021 | DDC 378.001--dc23

This paper meets the requirements of ANSI/NISO Z39.48-1992 (Permanence of Paper).

DEDICATION

I am dedicating this book to three very special people in my life. However, first and foremost I want to praise God and give him the glory and honor for guiding and leading me through this process.

I dedicate this book in honor and memory of my mother, my father, and my beloved wife, Sandy.

My mother's gentle spirit, unconditional love, and her abiding faith in God will always be an inspiration in my life.

My father was the best mentor and role model I ever had. He was truly a servant leader who practiced principle-centered leadership. Throughout my whole life, other than my God, I always wanted to be like him. When you read this book, you will know why.

Finally, my beloved wife, Sandy, was a true partner, and she provided stability in my life. Our unconditional love for each other was obvious to others. She recognized my weaknesses and helped me grow through her gentle reminders and unwavering candidness. Her strong faith, down-to-earth humility, and her quick wit will always be an inspiration and model for me.

TABLE OF CONTENTS

FOREWORD

Every once in a while, you encounter someone who just strikes you as extraordinary. Prakash is one of those special people. When you spend time with Prakash Mathew, you immediately feel valued. Prakash connects to you as a person, a professional, and a family member right from the first meeting and consistently every time you meet him. This very personal book explores his philosophy of leadership and the core beliefs and values that have been the foundation for his almost forty-year career in higher education. It encapsulates what makes Prakash extraordinary.

We Are Called examines the leadership and life philosophy of Prakash Mathew. A seasoned higher education leader, Prakash leads with his values. His belief in the goodness of others, his instinct as a teacher and counselor, his spiritual values, and his cultural heritage as a Desi-American all shaped over the course of more than four decades the ways in which he interacted with faculty, students, and staff while at North Dakota State University. Having served at NDSU for nearly forty years, Prakash also brings critical perspectives gleaned from working under eight college presidents and countless provosts, academic administrators, and student government officers. Here, Prakash speaks eloquently about the importance of understanding and exploring your core values and understanding the ways in which your personal values are congruent with the values of the institution and the leaders of that institution. This reckoning of values is a struggle for almost every leader no matter the industry.

Prakash is a respected leader in both higher education and his local community, which is evident by the way his work was recognized over his years as vice president for student affairs at North Dakota State University. Prakash lived the principles of being a servant leader, freely giving his time to NASPA— Student Affairs Administrators in Higher Education, and other community organizations. His commitment to the Fargo-Moorhead community in North Dakota has been long and deep. From serving as the president of the Fargo Public Library to serving in several community-based organizations, he understands the value of supporting the community surrounding NDSU. Nationally, he was deeply committed to NASPA having served on the NASPA Board of Directors and the NASPA Foundation Board of Directors. Prakash's student affairs peers awarded him the NASPA Pillar of the Profession in 2009, the NASPA Region IV West Distinguished Service Award in 2009, the James J. Rhatigan Outstanding Dean Award in 2014, and the NASPA Scott Goodnight Award for Outstanding Performance as a Dean in 2015. Through all these experiences, Prakash demonstrated his commitment to living his values with integrity and authenticity, two themes that are central to this book.

Prakash's experience at NDSU, from receiving a graduate degree to his long tenure as the vice president for student affairs provided a rich laboratory for him to explore and test his emerging theory of leadership. His impact on NDSU is unquestioned. Emblematic of the positive regard that NDSU had for Prakash was the decision by the North Dakota State Board of Higher Education to approve the renaming of NDSU's Living Learning Centers in honor of Prakash Mathew. The Living Learning Centers were designed specifically to bridge the living environments with the learning environments for students in this program, thus creating a holistic learning experience for the hundreds of students who participate annually and in recognition of the value of integrating where students live and learn.

Several years ago, I had the opportunity to conduct a presentation — hosted by Prakash — at NDSU. What I saw firsthand was his value-centric leadership in person with a constant focus on providing the best possible environment to support student engagement and students' development as successful citizens. Sometimes that means holding the line on institutional values when students engage in behavior that is inconsistent with institutional values. These are the hard decisions that Prakash never avoided. He viewed every interaction with a student, no matter the length, as a teachable moment. That was evident when I toured the NDSU campus with Prakash. Prakash was no "ivory-tower" administrator — I was in awe of how many students he knew on our walk around campus and how many students knew him. I could tell I was watching something special: a senior leader at a land-grant public university who knew most students on campus. In interviews with students who have graduated from NDSU, it is typical for alumni to refer to Prakash as the person at NDSU who singularly had an impact on their experience on campus. His student-focused leadership style is key to the way he approaches his work.

When asked about his connection to students, Prakash was clear about the core elements of these relationships: they were built on trust and authenticity. He was a real person to these students. He also looked at every interaction as an opportunity.

Enjoy Prakash's personal journey and exploration of leadership in the challenges and successes he experienced during his distinguished career at NDSU. There is a lot here to learn from as we all endeavor to be the best we can be as leaders, supervisors, and colleagues.

Kevin Kruger, PhD
President, NASPA—Student Affairs Administrators in Higher Education

ACKNOWLEDGMENTS

Writing a book was not on my radar in the early days of my career. When I was getting involved in my student affairs professional organization (NASPA), I started hosting workshops and retreats on various topics, particularly on the 80/20 Principle. As a result, many of my colleagues, staff, friends, and family strongly encouraged me to write this book. Since writing is not my strength, I had to solicit help from others to educate me about the book-writing process as well as to challenge me to think differently.

I am thankful to my sons Trevor and Chris Mathew and my daughter-in-law, Emily Mathew, for their love and support. I am so proud of their growth and development in their personal and professional lives. They, too, have taught me many life lessons and provided invaluable insights into various aspects of my book. My older son, Trevor, also served as one of the readers and editors of this book, and I am so grateful to him. My family is the most important priority in my life.

It is unbelievable how much God has blessed me with a new partner in my life, Jane. She was tremendously helpful in seeing this book project completed by sorting out my thoughts and feelings. I benefitted a great deal from her valuable insight. Jane and I were married on May 31, 2020. Let our journey continue!

Two of my former staff members, Casey Peterson and Deanne Sperling, also played a significant role in reading drafts of my book and providing their suggestions and edits, and I will always be grateful to them.

I give special thanks to Deanne for helping me complete this book through her undivided attention to editing and formatting, as well as providing much-needed clarity.

I did not have a title for this book until much later in the process. My friend Cortnee Jenson was instrumental in putting together a fascinating process to come up with a title. I am grateful to Cortnee.

Several people have made contributions in this book, and many of them are much better writers than I. I know you will enjoy reading their essays. You can find their names listed on their essays and their biographies listed on the contributors page. A reflection section from another colleague and friend is also included in chapter one. I am most grateful as well as indebted to them for their willingness, expertise, time, and above all, their friendship.

I have a special place in my heart for the students, staff, and faculty at North Dakota State University where I spent over three decades of my career. Many of them, particularly the students, became part of my extended family.

Thank you to First Presbyterian Church in Fargo for following God's call to generosity, welcoming me into your congregation, and giving me a spiritual home for nearly fifty years.

Finally, I want to honor all of my surrogate parents. I could not have made this journey without their love and guidance.

Forever I will be grateful for Vernon and Ruby Wold, Sandy's parents, and their family who adopted me and treated me as their own son.

Rev. Ross and Peg Robson, who gave me an opportunity by bringing me to this country for my graduate school in 1971.

Dr. Joel and Vivian Broberg, who provided my housing in Fargo until I married. Their family is very special to me.

To those of you who read this book, I want to thank and encourage you to make every effort in life to be a credible person and a leader. Remember, values are the glue that holds life's demanding details in place. I hope you enjoy reading *We Are Called*.

THE CALL:
MY PERSONAL STORY

Throughout my life, people have asked how I came to live in the United States and specifically in Fargo, North Dakota. It is not a simple story, but what you will see is that God was working overtime in my life. God planned my life's journey.

The Meeting That Changed Everything

I grew up as a Christian in India, a country where Hinduism is the majority religion, Islam the second largest, and Buddhism, Sikh, and Christian religions make up a very small minority. My father was a pastor in southern India in the state of Kerala.

In 1968, Pastor Ross and Peg Robson from the First Presbyterian Church in Fargo visited the college where I was pursuing my undergraduate degree. They were in India because of a Commission on the Ecumenical Missions and Relations of the Presbyterian Church. I was one of the student leaders selected to meet with the team of people from the United States, and I was paired up with Pastor Robson for a long interview. It was during this visit that I was asked if I had ever considered attending graduate school in the United States. I replied at the time, "It is in God's hands."

Even though it was not revealed to me until 1970, in that moment Pastor Robson had made a decision to bring me to the United States for my graduate degree at North Dakota State University (NDSU) in Fargo. Back in Fargo, Pastor Robson felt called to raise the funds needed to pay for my travel and tuition. It is through the generosity of First Presbyterian Church, Fargo, that this opportunity was provided to me.

I earned my degree in agricultural studies in India and began to prepare for the long and daunting trip to the United States. I said goodbye to my parents and siblings and left the country for the first time in September

1971. Travel from India to the United States was not easy, and I was more than a little nervous at the expected twenty-three hours of flight time. Leaving family and home for two years to begin graduate school was overwhelming. Due to the high cost and difficulty of travel, it was understood that I would not return home until I had completed my studies. Nevertheless, I felt that it was God's plan for me.

My Journey to the United States: At the Airport in New Delhi, India

I was sitting at the airport in New Delhi, India, waiting for my next flight connection. I began a conversation with a couple sitting next to me. We talked about our travel, and I shared my destination — Fargo, North Dakota. Much to our mutual shock, they were also from Fargo! They shared information about Fargo, and I was taking it all in. What a small world — was this God at work? Then they asked where I would be living. I told them I would be staying with Pastor Ross and Peg Robson. Again, another shocking coincidence! The couple informed me their daughter lived next door to the Robsons. Yes, this was definitely God's work!

My Journey to the United States: At JFK Airport, New York

I arrived in the United States at JFK Airport in New York, having traveled by myself, exhausted from days of travel and sleeping on airplanes and in airports. Yet, God continued his work and had another surprise for me. Standing at my gate at JFK Airport was none other than Pastor Robson and more than twenty church members who were just returning from an international trip. Based on my tentative itinerary, Pastor Robson had planned to meet me at JFK. What he did not tell me was that he would be traveling with a large group of church members. I felt such joy and comfort at being warmly greeted and welcomed by my new church family. They had been praying for me for the past two years and felt they knew me even though we had never met. On that trip, I met people who became my lifelong friends. Ross and Peg Robson became my second parents and took such good care of me. I became a part of their family, and they accepted me as their own son. They had made a commitment to my parents that they would watch over me and guide me while I studied in the United States. I have no doubt this was all part of God's plan for me.

My Introduction to Fargo, North Dakota

During the first week in Fargo, Dr. Joel and Vivian Broberg welcomed me into their home and provided me with housing until I completed my graduate studies. They loved and cared for me in every way possible, and they too became my surrogate parents. The love, support, and generosity of Joel and Vivian played a crucial role in my growth and development.

The generosity of First Presbyterian Church and the Robson and Broberg families was God's great gift to me. Nearly fifty years later, I still consider all of them my extended family. It is impossible for me to express my gratitude to Ross and Peg. None of this would have been possible without them finding me and bringing me to the United States. I truly believe it was indeed God's calling.

Meeting the Love of My Life, Sandy

I was in my second year of graduate studies and eating out with some friends. Across the restaurant, I noticed some other friends, so I went to say hello. A young lady I had never met before, Sandy Wold, was with them. We were both immediately drawn to each other. At the time, I had no plans to enter into a relationship, but we kept showing up at the same events, frequently hung out together, and finally, we began to date. Try to picture this: it was the '70s, and interracial marriage was not very common. Sandy was a beautiful Scandinavian woman with the lightest complexion and blond hair. I was a brown-skinned, dark-haired Indian man with an Indian accent. We were an unlikely couple. For one year, we met every week at a local restaurant. We got to know each other better while we drank coffee and took notes on paper napkins. Our relationship grew as we discussed our faith, values, cultural differences, and our families in Minnesota and India. We even contemplated how our children might look.

Our relationship grew closer, so I decided to write to my parents, asking for their blessing to marry Sandy. The most agonizing part for me was waiting for a response from my parents, which due to how slow the international mail was back then, took about a month. My family understood my great love for Sandy and gave their blessing to marry and for me to make my home in the United States. Later, I would learn more about their hesitation and concerns. They were concerned about the divorce rate in the United States. They were also disappointed because they were hoping that I would return home so that they could select a bride for me through a traditional arranged marriage. I am still overwhelmed by the love they showed us because this was certainly not how things were done in Indian culture.

———————   • • •   ———————

Our Wedding Day

In 1976, Sandy and I married at First Presbyterian Church in Fargo. Appropriately, Pastor Robson officiated our wedding, and both of our families were in attendance. My family loved Sandy and took her in as their own daughter. The Wolds took me into their family and accepted me fully as their son. I cherish the memories of Sandy's parents, Ruby and Vernon Wold, and their love was another one of God's great gifts to me.

> **God said to Abram, go from your country, your relatives, and your father's family, and go to the land I will show you. I will make you a great nation, and I will bless you. I will make you famous, and you will be a blessing to others. (Genesis 12:1-3)**

It is unbelievable how much God has blessed my life. Replicating Abram's call became a providence for answering God's call to me.

> **What does the Lord require of you but to do justice, and to love kindness, and to walk humbly with your God? (Micah 6:8)**

What was God's plan for me in Fargo? I was called to leadership. What was required of me was exactly as it is written in this often-quoted verse in Micah — through leadership, to humbly and lovingly work in ways to bring peacefulness and justice to the workplace.

So, I began my work in student affairs and found that the values and guiding principles that I learned from my parents were critical components of being a good leader. Yes, I was called to leadership. In my various student affairs roles — from a hall director position to North Dakota State University Vice President of Student Affairs — I had the joy and privilege to advise, mentor, and supervise many people. I worked hard to instill in students under my care the importance of knowing their own values and strongly-held principles so that they could become credible people. As a leader, it was my responsibility to make good decisions, implement organizational changes to better serve the students, create a positive culture, and model servant leadership for those entrusted to my care. As a supervisor, it was my objective to hire staff members who were a good fit with the values of NDSU. I instilled in them the importance of values, ethical leadership, and principles in their personal and work lives. In turn, I empowered them to create a positive culture and serve as role models for students and staff. I believe I also helped my peers and friends in navigating muddy waters by being a good friend who tried very hard to develop relationships built on values, honesty, and integrity.

Undoubtedly, God had a bigger plan for me. I may not always understand the plans for my life, but I am a firm believer that God sees the complete picture and has control of our journey. God has been at work in my life each and every day, and I was called to serve.

1

WE ARE CALLED TO LEADERSHIP

...

TO UPHOLD VALUES AS GUIDING PRINCIPLES

I have been approached by people to write a book about the principles and values that have been the guiding force in my life. In essence, this book is about the incredible values and principles I learned from my parents and the application of these values in my four decades of student affairs work in higher education. I believe these principles might be applicable to your personal and professional life as well as to managers and leaders across the world.

Values are the overarching theme of this book. Ever since I was a little boy, values and principles became part of my life, primarily because of my parents. My father was the most influential person in my life, and my mother was the most loving and compassionate person I have ever known.

I was born and raised in India, but our experiences may be very similar regarding listening to parental guidance. I respected my parents a great deal, and I lived my childhood listening to what they were teaching me without expressing any disagreement. My father often used to say, "It will be meaningful to you later in your life." His words proved true, and as a result, my parents became my heroes.

To help explain my story, it is important to understand that my parents were the best models in my entire life. They lived a remarkable life. My father was a tremendous leader. He was a man of influence. In fact, he was a pastor of the Church of South India, a Protestant denomination in Kerala, India. He was a true servant leader, practicing servant leadership in his everyday life. My father even had the great fortune to attend several prayer meetings with Mahatma Gandhi during the final years of the Independence Movement in India. My father's example of servant leadership may be why I ended up in the student affairs profession in higher education. Without question, I believe that student affairs professionals promote and teach servant leadership.

My mother also played a significant role in shaping and instilling my values. As I reflect on the personality of my mother, her humility, grace,

My father, Pastor C. G. Mathew

My mother, Chinnamma Mathew

Diligently
Studying the
Scriptures

warmth, and her faith in God stand out for me among the many qualities she possessed. She was a very traditional woman, and she accepted and respected my dad as the head of the household. Nevertheless, she played a significant supportive role in the church as well as in our community. I remember distinctly in my childhood days that she was particular about teaching us about the Sabbath day observance and expected us to stay home engaged in Bible reading or other non-work-related activities. We were not allowed to go out and play with friends in the neighborhood on Sundays, but she was never judgmental about their activities. She was loved and respected in all the communities where we lived. Her inclusiveness was admired by many, and she modeled this by inviting our Hindu and Muslim neighbors and friends to many of our Christian celebrations at our home, and we in in turn attended many religious celebrations at their homes. The influence of my mother remained with me throughout my life.

As I write this book about values, it is important for me to point out that my Christian faith and the mentoring of my parents played a huge role in shaping my values. I learned a great deal from their teachings and role modeling.

Early in my life, I used to think about my dad as the compass for my values. I remember asking myself when I was faced with challenging situations, what would my dad think or do? Even though his influence is woven through my life, my faith in God became a stronger part of my guiding principles and practices. With age, I started defining my life and identifying some core values that became part of my everyday living. Have I ever defaulted from my proclaimed values and principles? Of course! Whenever I have deviated from these values, I regretted it and paid a price for it later. As I learned from those mistakes and persisted in practicing those values, they became a part of my everyday life. Eventually, I did not have to think too hard when I was in a crisis mode or making an important decision. Often these pivotal values help define who I am as a person.

Let me set the stage with a compelling story that is still a vivid memory in my life. A widow with a young son needed a teaching job to support her family. I was in middle school at the time, and my father was a pastor of the Church of South India. He had responsibilities similar to those of a superintendent for all three levels of schools — elementary, middle, and high school — for a local parish in a small town in Kerala. Even though the woman was very qualified, there was a preference given to those of the same church denomination. The widow was passed over for a position many times.

Eventually, the woman became desperate enough that she sold all she had, took the money, and negotiated with the chief administrator of the church diocese, saying she would give them everything if they, in turn, would give her a position. The chief administrator agreed and proceeded to use the funds to build a classroom onto the school where my father was the pastor and superintendent. My father was thrilled that the woman was able to obtain a position but was very unhappy that the church diocese office took her money to secure this position.

As the addition neared completion, another teacher appeared at the Mathew residence/parsonage with the paperwork for his new position — to teach in the classroom recently added onto the school. My father was stunned and refused to sign the paperwork to finalize this post since the vacancy was already filled by the woman who provided her whole life savings to build the classroom addition.

Discussions with the diocese office went back and forth for some time. Finally, my father traveled to see the chief administrator and explained that this was simply not right for the church to accept this poor woman's money, and then not follow through with the promise. The chief administrator remained firm on his stand. My father presented two options for the diocese to consider: return the money in full to the teacher or take the school addition down and sell the materials to return her money. If these options were not acceptable, he would resign from his role as superintendent and pastor of his parish.

Since the church members and bishop thought very highly of my father, the congregation unanimously shot down the option of him resigning and the bishop would not allow him to quit. Once again, everything was at a standstill.

My father returned to the town, and the local church members — along with my father — organized a community effort to take apart the school addition. The school was up on a hill. A line was formed from the school to the parsonage where, shoulder to shoulder and piece by piece, the school addition was taken apart. All the building supplies were passed down the line and then stacked in the front yard so they could be sold and the funds returned to the widow. The school addition was removed in one day. It was a true community event.

The bishop and the chief administration arrived and saw what had happened. Finally, the diocese made the right decision to keep both positions and add onto the school — one classroom for the widow and the other classroom for the new teacher who was still living at the parsonage.

Another community event was planned, and the people stood shoulder to shoulder to rebuild the school.

This story displays the convictions and principles of my father. He was truly a principle-centered servant leader. He was a preacher who always followed through in practicing what he preached. He did not do this to prove a point, nor did he do this as a heroic act. He simply wanted to do the right thing for the right reason.

Values

So, what are values? Values are firmly held beliefs people support and act from. Values are the guiding principles that define the character of a leader.

What we do in our everyday lives should reflect our values and beliefs. To clarify our values, we need to ask these questions:

- What do I believe in?
- What are my guiding principles?
- What governs my life?
- What is my moral compass?
- What do I stand for?

Your personal convictions will determine how you live your life. Rather than waiting for someone else to define your beliefs, decide what principles and values you will live by. What is your moral compass, what governs your life, what do you stand for? Ask yourself regularly, what is the right thing to do? Remember, values are the glue that holds life's demanding details in place and will help you discover who you are as a person.

Very early in my career I clarified the core values in my life:

- Honor God by strengthening my relationship
- Model a loving, trusting, and respectful relationship with my family and friends
- Do the right thing for the right reason
- Practice principle-centered servant leadership
- Practice stewardship in my personal and professional life

It is important for all of us to go through a process to identify values. There is growth involved with all these values, and I was not the same man in my early days as I am now.

Our human tendency is to do what is convenient and popular because we want to be accepted or liked. There is never a wrong time to do the right thing, and it is always important to do the right thing for the right reason. This was my father's message, and it always echoed in my ear. I would like to share a principle I have found valuable for decades of my life. I call it the 80/20 Principle.

— 2 —

WE ARE CALLED TO LEADERSHIP
...
TO PRACTICE
THE 80/20 PRINCIPLE

For almost twenty-five years in my professional career, I have been talking about a concept called the 80/20 Principle, which I shared with literally hundreds of people during workshops, training sessions, one-on-one meetings, and keynote presentations. I have wanted to put this in writing for a long time, but other priorities in my personal life and work delayed this process. Friends, colleagues, and employees have all encouraged me to write this book. Some of them have given testimonies on how this principle has helped them personally and professionally. In fact, I received an e-mail from a person that I once interviewed for a position, who jokingly said he would use the principle and write the book if I did not. He told me he has been using this principle often in his workplace. It crossed my mind that by the time that I write this book, most people in my profession may have heard about this concept already, and they could even question the credibility of its origin.

Strategy, System, and Values

The following principle provides the framework to utilize when making decisions every day in our workplaces.

Stephen Covey's book *Principle-Centered Leadership* talks about an analogy to describe our work with people in an organization: Give a man a fish, and you feed him for a day; teach him how to fish, and you feed him for a lifetime. The origin of this adage is highly contested, with possible sources being Chinese, Native American, Indian, or biblical. Regardless of its origin, the phrase sets an excellent framework for this part of my discussion. The goal is always to teach people how to fish the stream for themselves. The stream represents the environments, the ever-changing realities we face in an organization. So, how should we deal with it? As Stephen Covey suggests, three ingredients may be beneficial: strategy, system, and shared values. I am sure all of you understand why strategy is an essential element. This is the reason why most organizations go through the strategic planning process. How about system? Most of us struggle with system. I struggled with the system, particularly when I worked with the university systems in Minnesota and North Dakota. Systems often create bureaucracy, but they can also provide consistency, order, and organization. The third ingredient, values, guides us in the journey. This ingredient is our compass.

A former president at a university where I worked expanded the internal auditor's office shortly after his arrival and renamed it the Office of Ethics, Compliance, and Audit. He said it sends a message. What is that message? Most of us are good at complying with rules and regulations, but it is much more than that. He was encouraging us to ask the question, what is the right thing to do? The prompt helped the campus create a culture regarding ethical behavior in our decision-making process. There are many streams with differing currents that affect the success of our organizations. When strategy, system, and shared values within your organization are in harmony with the streams, it is more likely that the team will achieve success.

Application of the 80/20 Principle to Personal and Organizational Values

What happens when your personal values conflict with your organizational values? This is where the 80/20 Principle comes into play. When a per-

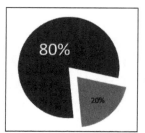

The Basic 80/20 Principle

son's values conflict with the institutional values more than 20 percent of the time, you are in a discomfort zone. In other words, you will go home stressed out. You may be miserable. Remember, you are never going to find a 100 percent match in any organization. Most of us also have certain values we will not compromise. At the same time, we also need to make some compromises. In some cases, we can make those compromises, and in other situations, we cannot. When we are not able to make compromises, and we feel we cannot live with our conscience, then we may have to make a hard choice or find an organization that is a better fit.

Application of the 80/20 Principle to the Job Search

We all have choices to make. Sometimes when we are going through the job search process, and think we really want the job, we do not do enough research about the organization's values or ask the right questions. It is easy to get into a situation where our desire for the job makes it difficult for us to turn down a position. Often the consequences might be too great, so we shy away from doing the right thing for the right reason.

It is crucial to research the mission and values of the organization before accepting a position. If you can identify your guiding principles, then you will be able to match with the organization's values. During an interview process, it is equally important for an individual to ask about an organization's values and their application, and in the same way, it is important for the organization to understand the values of the individual.

As you go through the job search process, if you believe your values conflict with the organization's, particularly those values that are very close to your core, then you may need to make a decision at a very early stage if you will move forward with the process. Most people do not consider this option when they are looking for a job; people are only focusing on finding a job. So, many times, individuals are already sacrificing their values to meet their personal goal.

When you are hired, if you find yourself in a predicament where more than 20 percent of situations are difficult for you to manage based on the conflict between your personal values and the institutional values, this may be a time when you need to evaluate if these conflicts are normal processes in the organization. The higher the percentage of discomfort or difficulty, the more acute the problem you will encounter. You have to decide what conflicts of values you can live with and what are the values where you cannot compromise. As I noted before, it is impossible to find a position where there is a 100 percent match with the organization. Your goal should be to gel with the team so you are useful and productive. If you believe in the values and mission of the organization without a struggle on a regular basis, your effectiveness will be optimal. As you work with the team for a period, there is a possibility for you to narrow the discomfort zone to less than 20 percent.

Most of us want to be liked or popular. In this situation, again, we have a tendency not to speak up, and we compromise our values. We may frequently avoid doing the right thing for the right reason because we fear the impact of our actions.

The assumption is that because you are compromising your values, the organization is doing something wrong. This belief is not always the case. Sometimes, the employee may be the one who needs to change when the organization is on the right track. Whether it is the employee or the organization, the goal is to bring the discomfort zone closer to 10 percent.

I worked at North Dakota State University (NDSU) for a very long time, and I believe that my discomfort zone was less than 10 percent throughout my career. I left NDSU for a short period to work at another great university. During the first year at this new institution, there was no question that I had to do something to reduce my discomfort zone, which was beyond 20 percent. Even though I felt most of the staff seemed to be doing OK within the department regarding the policies and procedures, I was in a discomfort zone. Many weeks I went home burdened with the decisions made at the university, which I had to support and implement. At the same time, I knew very well that I was compromising my values. Since I was holding a senior administrative position, I had the authority to change the culture, to turn it around to satisfy my needs. I thought about this several times, and I was tempted to make these changes, but I realized that by doing this I was changing their culture and their discomfort zone to a wider margin. Instead, I had conversations about my viewpoints based on my values and principles. I was making an impact on them through my actions, behaviors, and results. This took time. Within two years, through several discussions, I believe that I reduced my discomfort zone to somewhere in the ballpark of 15 percent.

In this situation, I was in a position to make necessary changes within the department. At the same time, I did not want to be viewed as a hard-nosed outsider, coming in and making changes and doing things my way. So, I tried to make a cultural transformation, which took a longer period.

The fit between your values and the organization's values has been shown to be a predictor of job satisfaction and attrition for the organization. How can the organization's values fit into your personal values and vice versa? What happens when there are conflicts? Is there a way that you can find common ground or a win-win situation?

A while ago when I was making a presentation on this topic, someone asked me how I came up with the 20 percent threshold for the discomfort zone. For some of you this 20 percent range might be too liberal, and you might fall within a 10 to 15 percent range. Each of us needs to make this judgment as our own. It is perfectly appropriate to adjust this range based on your personal values and principles. The 20 percent range I selected is based on extensive conversations with many staff members with whom I worked over the years as well as professional colleagues across the nation. Upon becoming familiar with this concept, I asked them to describe their discomfort zone range and a majority of them selected 20 percent.

———————   • • •   ———————

A Personal Reflection on the 80/20 Principle and Its Application

By Dr. Eric Grospitch, Vice President for Student Affairs, Washburn University

Sitting in a meeting of the NASPA IV-West Advisory Board in the early 2000s, I had the opportunity to hear from our new Regional Vice President, Prakash Mathew, as he shared his vision for the region and for NASPA. As he laid out his groundwork for our next two years working together, Prakash began to explain what he referred to as the 80/20 Principle. As a new professional, it resonated with me, but at that time I did not realize exactly how important it would become in my professional career.

As my career has progressed, I often reflect upon that first conversation and how I continue to apply the rule to any decision that I have made regarding my fit at an institution. Questions like: Do my values align with the institution's values? Or with the president's values? Does the institution support and encourage programs that support those values? How are critical decisions made? When things get difficult, what values are strongest? And ultimately, Can I make a difference here? Throughout my career, I have used these questions and many like them to decide the next steps in either problem solving or in career moves. It is this last one for which I will provide some context.

I had the opportunity to work at an institution where leadership spoke strongly about the importance of the student experience and creating a vibrant campus community for students from all backgrounds. I found this environment to be exciting and energizing. I thrived there both professionally and personally. However, there were leadership changes and decisions that were made that started to make me question the institutional values and the values of those that I worked for. I began to see colleagues that no longer seemed interested in what was best for the students but were interested in what was best for their own area or personal agendas, and the students started to suffer. Basic supports that were needed for students were seen as taxes on the academic units, and programs that supported the success and retention of diverse students began to be seen as burdens. Student Affairs began to be seen as simply the firefighters for student flashpoints, and we were expected to keep everything in its place.

As more and more of these experiences happened, I struggled to understand why I was personally feeling so poorly. It was not until I remembered Prakash's 80/20 Principle that I recognized what had happened. My values were no longer at least 80 percent in line with my organization's actions, and I was suffering. I was convinced that I could make changes to bring back the energy that I had felt before, but the work environment continued to be at odds with my values. While it took me a year to come to that realization, probably because I did not really want to, I eventually determined it was time to leave before the environment changed me.

Three years into my new role, I have found an environment that not only matches my values, but colleagues that are working together to live those values as a university. Any chance that I get to work with colleagues as they discern their professional paths, I share with them the importance of the 80/20 Principle and finding the environment they can be successful in and that matches their individual values. This match allows decisions that you make to improve the campus and the environment to be in congruence with each other, thus increasing the likelihood that those decisions will lead to the success of the project, program, or person.

One thing that I learned, however, is that no place will ever have a 100 percent value agreement as long as we are dealing with humans. I found that it is not only necessary to realize that some decisions will be made that fundamentally are in conflict with your values, you also have to be able to find paths to work with and through those situations. The 80/20 Principle is not about being offended or not liking an answer. To me it is about recognizing intent and impact of decisions and determining if this was truly a core value issue, or simply a disagreement.

• • •

Authors James M. Kouzes and Barry Z. Posner, in *Credibility: How Leaders Gain and Lose It, Why People Demand It*, talk about employees' loyalty to the organization when they believe their values and those of the organization are aligned. They also discuss how the quality and accuracy of communication and the integrity of the decision-making process increases when people feel part of the same team.

In their research involving more than one thousand managers in a range of different companies and industries, they found that:

> **those who shared their business's shared values and experienced congruency between their personal values and those of their company reported significantly more positive attachments to their work and organization than those who felt that little relationship existed. These two groups, not surprisingly, also differed in the extent to which they found their management to be credible.**[1]

Differences and obstacles are often found regarding alignment of personal and organizational values. The first step is to explore our own inner territory, so that we are clear about what is important to us.

Application of the 80/20 Principle to the Decision-Making Process

Another way to apply the 80/20 Principle is in your decision-making process. How do we create a process to help feed for a lifetime? What happens when every time we encounter a problem, we run to the supervisor or manager for fish? Since this manager is also supervised by other managers and supervisors, they work in a constant problem-solving or management-by-crisis mode. Here again, apply the 80/20 Principle to assess the situation before you move forward.

My recommendation is that every person in an organization should have the responsibility and authority to make decisions for 80 percent of the items listed in their job description. If they are not empowered to do this, I believe there is a micro-management problem in that organization. At the same time, some of the staff members unjustly blame the organization's management for micro-management when they are unhappy with their supervisor or their position. Most of the time, it may not be a micro-management problem. So, it is important for every employee to look

---

[1]James M. Kouzes and Barry Z. Posner, *Credibility: How Leaders Gain and Lose It, Why People Demand It* (John Wiley & Sons, Inc: 2011), p. 122.

at their job description and determine if they have the responsibility and ownership to make 80 percent of the decisions. Also, look to see what decisions are made beyond your departmental level.

Application of the 80/20 Principle in Personal Relationships

As a rule of thumb, we search for a partner to share our life. So, how do you know you are compatible? As a couple, it is important to know your values align. Often, people fall in love and get married for various reasons without making a concerted effort to make sure there is an alignment of values in their life so their relationship will not end up in separation or divorce.

Let me set the stage by talking about my beloved wife, Sandy, and how we aligned our values prior to our marriage. We were married for over forty years. Heartbreakingly, she passed away in 2017. Sandy spent several months at multiple hospitals, including Mayo Clinic in Rochester, Minnesota. During her stay, there was one question that was repeatedly asked by staff: "What is the secret to our marriage?" Our love for each other was very strong, and this was evident to others.

So, let us start with how it all began. Over forty years ago, we were each attending separate universities across the river from each other. We first met at a local family restaurant, and we had a strong connection. It was also a thoughtful and calculated process as we progressed in our relationship. She was a blond, blue-eyed, beautiful Scandinavian descendant from Minnesota, and I was born in southern India. Despite the geographic differences in our upbringing, we shared a Christian faith and many common values and principles.

When we realized our relationship was more serious than we anticipated, we hit the pause button. We both agreed that we needed to make sure we understood each other. We designated time each week to ask each other some tough questions. I remember having many conversations, with coffee and pie, where we would write our thoughts and concerns on restaurant napkins. We talked about our race, color, religion, culture, faith, values, and principles. We also spoke of any possible objections from our parents. I distinctly remember in one of those meetings we even talked about what our children might look like and if they would be accepted in the conservative society in which we were living.

We were both very close to our families, so we agreed that before making any serious commitment to each other, we needed the consent and

Sandy Wold Mathew

blessings of our parents. I was brought up within the tradition of arranged marriages where your parents picked your bride for you. When we spoke with our parents, we learned that my parents were concerned about the divorce rate in the United States and her parents were concerned about my faith and religion. Since Sandy grew up as a farmer's daughter in northern Minnesota, I thought their objections might have been with my race or other cultural barriers. I was pleasantly surprised to find out their main concern was with my faith. With my parents, I knew they felt very strongly about marriage being a lifelong commitment, so we openly talked about the principles and values involved in our wedding vows. Even though we loved each other very much, we talked for over a year to make sure there was an alignment of our values. This alignment of values proved to be true throughout our marriage.

Application of the 80/20 Principle in Politics

Value alignment also applies in political situations. In many countries across the globe, as part of their political structure, governing officials often struggle to form a majority government after an election. When a political party does not have the majority seats needed to form a government, it often reaches out to other opposing parties to form a coalition government even though their philosophical base may be on the opposite ends of the spectrum. As a result, the government's stability is jeopardized with the possibility of collapse. In this situation, political parties are compromising their values to gain power and positions in the government even though they are fully aware of the disconnect within their parties. A disconnect between political parties and leadership seems to be a common occurrence even in our own country. Political leaders are compromising or sacrificing their principles and values to align with their political parties rather than dealing with issues that are brought before them.

Looking at politics in the United States, an important lesson could be learned from the 80/20 Principle. If Americans were to focus on the things that we all agree upon — the importance of free speech, education, good health care, and safety are all examples — we would be focusing on the 80 percent. We would be a stronger country if we focused on this positive part of what binds us together as a great country. Instead, our country spends a large amount of energy focusing on the 20 percent about which we disagree. As a country, we have allowed political parties and biased reporting to convince us that there is more than 20 percent discomfort.

3

WE ARE CALLED TO LEADERSHIP

...

TO BECOME
A CREDIBLE PERSON

We are engaged in shaping and influencing the lives of people every single day. This means that you are a person of influence. How do you do this? Before we can do any work shaping the lives of others, I am a firm believer that we must shape our own lives. If you were to author your own personal and professional story, what would it say?

To become a person of influence, you can use these four principles as a guide: Who, What, How, and Why. We all have different stories to tell based on our varied backgrounds and experiences, and how we may connect the dots in our life may also be very different. Let me help you pave your path for the future as you write your own personal and professional story. As I mentioned, there are four principles that I want to explain, and the first is *who* you are.

**Four Principles
of Becoming a
Credible Person**

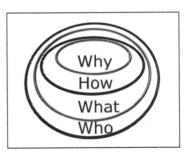

Who?

Most of the time, you are selected for your job primarily because of your skills and attributes. But it takes more. To be a good leader, a person of influence, and a credible leader, you must know what you believe in, what your values are, and what it is that makes you tick. If you want to be a good leader, you must know who you are! Rather than waiting for someone else to offer direction or write your story, decide for yourself what principles and values you will live by.

These questions will help you clarify your values:

- What do I believe in?
- What are my guiding principles?
- What governs my life?
- What do I stand for?
- Ask yourself constantly: What is the right thing to do?

Why is this so critical? Now, I do not want to make assumptions about how comfortable you are with knowing and being able to state your values. This was a common topic of discussion around the dinner table at our house when our two sons were growing up. I firmly believe that you will not be able to move forward successfully until you know who you are as a person. There is an excellent book by Parker Palmer called *Let Your Life Speak: Listening for the Voice of Vocation*. "Let your life speak" means before you tell what you intend to do or what truths and values you have decided to live up to, let your life tell what truths you embody and what values you represent.

To demonstrate this a little further as to *who you are*, I want to describe two stories from my life. In this first story, I learned the hard way some valuable lessons about sharing at a young age. I grew up in southern India in a state called Kerala. At the time of this story, I was in first grade. One day, I was with my family at a harvest festival. At this festival, I bought a pineapple using money my parents gave me. I was very proud of my purchase. I wanted to eat this pineapple all by myself, and I did not want to share with my younger brother and older sisters. My parents asked why I didn't want to share the pineapple and I replied, "I bought this pineapple with my own money."

So, my father very wisely and very quietly said to my mother, "I believe Prakash bought the pineapple, and the pineapple should be his. He doesn't want to share, so he will eat the whole pineapple." My mother sat me down at the table, cut up the pineapple, and as my brothers and sisters watched me, I ate and ate and ate.

Well, soon I began to feel a little guilty as I sat there, all alone, while others watched. And, besides, I was getting full. So, I offered to share the pineapple with my brother and sisters. But my father insisted, "No, it is Prakash's pineapple, and he does not wish to share it. He will finish eating the pineapple all by himself." And so, I forced myself to continue eating, and I finished.

Can you guess what happened to me? The acid of the pineapple made my mouth so sore that I had difficulty eating for several days. My father knew this. He was teaching me a valuable lesson about sharing and serving others even at a young age. Sometime later, my father took me aside and explained the most important part of this lesson. Together, we planted the top from the same pineapple. I nurtured the tiny plant for months. When the pineapple was fully grown and ripened — with great gratitude and humility — I gifted it back to church for the same festival. My father taught me a valuable lesson about giving and sharing. My dad was a very wise man. I never forgot this important lesson which has become a significant value in my life.

The second story is about learning not to lie ever again. I have a distinct memory of this incident even though I was only five years old. My family had a beautiful wooden tea table in our living room that we used occasionally to serve afternoon tea for our guests. Afternoon tea was a British tradition that we followed in India. We had a big seashell displayed on that table. One day, my parents went out for a few hours and gave the responsibility to my older sisters to take care of my brother and me. Soon after they left, I decided to pick up the seashell and accidentally dropped it on the table and made some dents. Suddenly a crazy thought occurred to me to make more marks and be creative. I decided to pound the shell on the table over and over again, making dents in anticipation of creating an imaginary design. In the end, I practically destroyed the beautiful table. A few minutes later, my oldest sister walked into the room and noticed what I was doing. She was shocked and forewarned me about the possible consequence from my parents. Upon their arrival, my father instantly noticed the damage, and he scanned our faces and immediately focused his attention on me. He gently and firmly asked me if I was responsible for the damage. My immediate reaction was to lie, and I responded "no." My father repeated the question again even more firmly. I lied once again with some fear and tears in my eyes. As he was asking the question the third time, I started running. My father grabbed me, put me on his lap, and held me tightly. This time I admitted that I was responsible. My dad, with firm and tender care, explained to me that I should always tell the truth regardless of how difficult or large the consequence might be. Even though I was very young, this significant event made an impact in my life. I will never forget the lesson my father taught me about lying. Almost forty years later, when our family visited India, I was able to show this table to my sons. This is a story that I will never forget because this incident made a mark, or should I say a *dent*, in my life.

Each one of us has our own experiences, and no two stories are alike. These experiences explain who we are as people.

Who You Are as a Person Clarifies Values and Beliefs

Remember, values are the glue that holds life's demanding details in place; values will play a primary role as you author your own story. We all know that understanding who you are as a person helps you identify your beliefs and values.

I would like to share with you a compelling story that describes the conscience as existing in the form of a triangle, a sharp, three-cornered stone located deep within the heart. Whenever values are violated, the stone revolves or turns. With each turn, the corners cut you and hurt your soul (or heart). If values continue to be violated, sooner or later the sharp corners of the stone will be rounded off, and the conscience will no longer "cut" as it should.

The concept of the conscience being worn down whenever values are violated provides an insightful explanation of world events in our society. Again, who you are as a person helps you identify your beliefs and values.

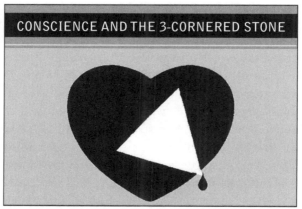

Conscience and the Three-Cornered Stone

What?

The next principle is *what* you are. This concept is about critically assessing your knowledge and your skills. Are you engaging in opportunities where you can learn and grow? Are you improving your knowledge base? I am not only talking about your current knowledge here; I am also talking about challenging yourself daily with new insight, developing your people skills, and building relationships.

You might be wondering how I put this into practice in my own career. When I began my career in student affairs, I managed to connect with all the hall directors and resident assistants by posting their photos and names on my wall. Whenever I would go for my weekly visits, I would usually review and memorize the names. It made such a difference when I could call a staff member by name. I put the challenge back to them and challenged them to memorize all the names of the residents on their floor or hall. I continued to practice this throughout my life. I took pride in remembering names of hundreds of students and staff that I met in my professional career. This is just one example of how we must be intentional about building relationships and strengthening interpersonal skills.

So, how do you change or strengthen what you are? You do this by setting goals and developing action plans so you are always learning and growing in your knowledge and skills. Personally, I set aside time every week to either read a new book or journal article, or to write about leadership. It is critical that we stay on top of the latest trends and news. You might think that those advanced in their profession no longer need to improve their skills or knowledge. I can tell you, there is nothing further from the truth.

What you are is the focus of a familiar story (source unknown) about a young woman who went to her mother and told her that she didn't know how she was going to make it and wanted to give up. She was struggling and faced with one problem after another. Her mother took her to the kitchen, filled three pots with water, and filled the first one with carrots, the second with eggs, and the third with ground coffee beans. She let them each boil for about twenty minutes. She turned off the burners and took the carrots, eggs, and coffee out and placed them in separate bowls. She asked the daughter to feel each of them separately. The carrots were soft and a little mushy, the eggs were hard and no longer breakable, and the coffee beans had a rich aroma.

Her mother explained to her daughter that these three objects had faced the same obstacle, the boiling water, but each reacted differently.

"Which one are you?" the mother asked the daughter, "a carrot, egg, or coffee bean?" When you face a difficulty in life, how do you respond? This story brings into focus the need to work on our skills and knowledge to confront the obstacles of life. Are you a carrot that seems strong, but with adversity you wilt and become soft and lose your internal strength? Are you an egg that changes with heat and becomes hardened and stiff? Or, are you like the coffee bean, and when placed in the heat release fragrance and flavor, making the best of a challenging situation? When I talk about these first two principles — *who* you are and *what* you are — I want to be clear that these areas will continue to evolve and change as you progress in your careers.

How?

The next principle is *how*. How are you living your life? This is where the rubber hits the road. It seems like a simple question, but honestly, this is probably the most difficult one. To help you process your answer, I would like you to consider two more questions.

Are you making good choices? I am not asking you to be perfect, but what I am asking you to do is live your values. This is where your values and convictions in life become a reality and where it must be second nature to do the right thing for the right reason. Sometime in your life — you can count on it — your values will be tested.

Are you staying on the right path? This is where you practice what you preach. Your values must be a part of your everyday life so you do not have to think twice before you act. I am sure you have heard the saying that there is never a wrong time to do the right thing. Remember, as adults, we do not have room for many excuses. Most of us have good intentions, but we do not always put them into action. Our human tendency is to take the easy way out and do what is convenient or most comfortable. Often, this is motivated by wanting to be liked. This leads us to the route that is popular.

Making Tough Decisions for the Right Reasons

In the midpoint of my career as Dean of Student Life, I encountered a very challenging situation, and I want to share this story with you. Like many institutions, there was a problem with alcohol use in our Greek houses. The problem was significant enough that a committee had met for over a year, thoroughly reviewed the problem, yet came up with no solution. For me, this was simply unacceptable. I also knew that the subject was a political hot button and a problem that needed to be tackled. With the support of the president and my vice president, I put together a group representing current Greek students, Greek alumni, faculty, staff, and non-Greek students. After several months of study, we presented a plan that included several goals and strategies for how to address the issue of alcohol in the Greek houses. I made a list of all the people that I needed to convince. This list included some influential alumni. Over the course of several years, I had breakfasts and lunches with forty-three different stakeholders and laid out the university's plan to implement an alcohol policy. There were numerous steps I went through. I also contacted the national Greek organizations and gained their endorsement. Finally, we implemented a new alcohol policy. Initially, some of the Greek students were not very happy, and I was not very popular either. But we believed it was the right thing to do for our students. Our Greek houses are now stable, and alcohol incidences are under control. I was invited back to their houses often for their programs and activities as well as their Monday night dinners. What is the significance of this story? Sometimes in our lives, we need to make tough decisions for the right reasons, even if it is not the popular thing to do. Folks, you will never lose respect for doing the right thing. Remember, changing the culture is never easy.

You should also speak out for what you believe. There is a difference between being judgmental and standing up for what you believe. But you can only speak out for what you believe after you put your values into action. Always follow the golden rule of treating others the way you want to be treated, and do not set expectations for others that you yourself are not practicing.

Here are some of the words that are commonly associated with how:

- commitment
- honesty
- accountability
- respect
- courage
- ethics

These are all strong, powerful words.

Now, I would like to share another story as described by Parker Palmer in *Let Your Life Speak* about one of the great heroes of our time, Rosa Parks:

Many years after the famous bus encounter, a graduate student came to Rosa Parks and asked, "Why did you sit down

at the front of the bus that day?" Rosa Parks said, "I sat down because I was tired." She meant that her soul, her heart, and her whole being was tired. But in the moment she sat down at the front of the bus, she set in motion a process that changed both the lay and the law of the land. She decided "I will no longer act on the outside in a way that contradicts the truth that I hold deeply on the inside. I will no longer act as if I were less than the whole person I know myself inwardly to be."[2]

This is how you must strive to live your life. This story demonstrates perfectly the how in leadership.

Why?

The final principle I would like you to think about is the concept of the *why* of what you do. In my opinion, this is the most important concept.

What is the *why* of your organization? Let me explain. In the early days of my career when I was involved in staff training, I remember our staff were primarily interested in learning about the how-to part of their work. They often asked me to show them what to do and how to do it. Yes indeed, those things were important tasks, but I reminded them that even more important was the why of what they did.

While I served as the vice president for Student Affairs, each summer I held a retreat for the directors in Student Affairs and one year, as a group, we watched a Ted Talk video.[3] We watched the Simon Sinek Ted Talk about how great leaders inspire action. What is so intriguing about Simon's talk is that he challenges people to think about how we communicate the why of what we do, what is our purpose, what is our cause, and what is our belief?

Most people easily articulate what it is they do. At a university, staff work with students. They provide services and programs to students and may engage in decisions holding them accountable for their actions. They also help students develop skills that will help them get through college and into adulthood. But the part that is most difficult is being able to make the next connection to articulate the why.

Simon Sinek's theory that has resonated with more than forty-three million people is that people do not connect with you over what you do

---

[2] Parker J. Palmer, *Let Your Life Speak: Listening for the Voice of Vocation* (San Francisco: John Wiley & Sons, 1999), p. 32.
[3] Original Simon Sinek Ted Talk link:
https://www.ted.com/talks/simon_sinek_how_great_leaders_inspire_action?utm_
campaign=tedspread&utm_medium=referral&utm_source=tedcomshare

or how you do it. They connect with you about why. My purpose is to get you thinking about the *why* of your job, and specifically how you could do a better job if you are able to articulate the why of your job.

On this topic, I gave a presentation to Student Affairs staff and gave everyone a business card. On one side was a huge WHY and on the other side it said TO MAKE A DIFFERENCE IN THE LIVES OF THE STUDENTS. This was immediately popular because it got right to the heart of the reason for our work. Imagine my surprise when other departments and individuals who otherwise had little interest in student affairs work also connected with the message on the cards.

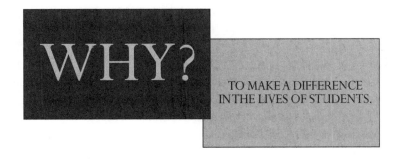

As you think about who, what, how, and why of leadership, I would like to personally challenge each of you to be a credible person of influence and a servant leader. For me, there is no other way to live. If we live our life with serving as our priority, we can make a difference in this world by setting an example for others to follow.

How Do You Describe a Credible Leader?

Most of us know and understand all the right principles to be a credible leader, but our failures come from not practicing these principles. So, how can you become a credible leader? Our ability to influence others is based on our personal qualities as well as our knowledge, competence, experience, etc., which can be described as skills.

If you were asked to give names of some credible people of influence in your life, I am sure you would be able to name them without much problem. Why did you select these people? What are the qualities of these people? My father happens to be the person who had the most impact in my life, so he is number one on my list. Most of us are able to identify these people because they were credible people. How do you know someone is credible?

If you were to write down all the human qualities most necessary for a leader to lead an organization, what do you think will be on the top of the list? Authors Barry Posner and James Kouzes in their book *Leadership Challenge* talk about a study they did among thirteen hundred executives showing that 71 percent put integrity on the top of the list.

I am also in agreement that the most important ingredient of leadership is integrity. Our words and our actions must match up. John Maxwell's book, *Developing the Leader Within You*, talks a great deal about credibility in leadership. Integrity also builds trust. To earn trust, a leader must first establish relationships with people. In my opinion, the relationships are the key to our success and for any organization.

Organizations and people spend a lot of time working to protect image more than integrity. What is the difference between image and integrity? Is there a difference? Image is who people think we are, and integrity is who we really are. There are attributes, skills, and knowledge necessary to become a credible person. We also talked about how you live your life by demonstrating your values and utilizing the 80/20 Principle.

Two primary components play a crucial role in your development as a credible person. Number one is your personal qualities. The second component is your skills. Your competence, knowledge, and experience play a role to enhance this element. It is essential to have personal qualities balance with competency or skills; one without the other is ineffective.

How do you know someone is credible?

Personal Qualities

Skills
Knowledge
Experience

Finding Balance as a Credible Person

First, let me suggest some areas we can explore to strengthen our life so that you become that quality person. Some examples I will mention are personal attributes or characteristics such as integrity, excellence, attitude, and authenticity. Similarly, let me identify the other half: skills, knowledge, etc. I have prioritized and narrowed the areas down to four I believe are critical: communication, decision-making, self-discipline, and relationships. Your list may be different than mine.

As I mentioned earlier, being a credible person requires a balance between personal qualities and competency.

4

WE ARE CALLED TO LEADERSHIP

...

TO BE A

DECISION-MAKER

How do we make decisions in our life? Some people process things intellectually and objectively using their head and then pulling the trigger with their heart. Others deal with emotional issues first using their heart to process things and then making the decisions with their head. I do not believe there is a right or wrong way to make decisions.

Children learn at a very early stage to make decisions by watching their parents, asking the why questions, testing their boundaries, and learning what is right and wrong. They also learn how certain decisions are made and the consequence to these decisions. Let me share how my wife Sandy and I instilled values and decision-making skills through modeling for our children. As our two sons were growing up, there were family meetings once or twice a week at the dinner table. It was an opportunity to get them involved in sharing ideas and feelings about life in general as well as dealing with matters impacting them every single day, such as responsibilities, boundaries, curfews, etc. We established boundaries, but they had input in everything. They could bring suggestions for changes and lobby for their argument. Believe it or not, sometimes they convinced us that we were not always reasonable or did not have a good rationale for our rules. We taught them simple parliamentary procedures allowing them to bring their ideas and present them as a motion. Of course, Sandy and I voted on their motion after a brief discussion. Often, their proposal was approved with the understanding of the consequences if they did not comply with what they promised. Through this process, our sons learned at an early age that freedom and responsibility go hand in hand, and that if they wanted to have freedom, they needed to take responsibility. We also taught them that as parents, we were also accountable to the established standards. These meetings provided opportunities to be role models for appropriate behavior and to practice what we preached. Now, many years later in our family conversations, our sons often reflect on the relationship Sandy and I established with them at these dinner meetings. These are cherished memories.

We all appreciate the choices available to us and the opportunities to make decisions about those choices. We seek to shape our destiny. Like many parents, Sandy and I may have been overbearing at times, but we hope we guided our sons when they needed some direction in their lives. I believe we can also say with some certainty that we gave them the freedom to choose their lifestyle based on the knowledge, tools, and values they gained throughout their lives. Since life is a journey, they will pick and choose as well as develop their own principles and values in their lives.

For most managers, making decisions is not an easy process. Of course, there are some easy decisions, but many decisions require input from others, review of the pros and cons, or extensive research. Often times, decisions are not made in a timely manner or sometimes members of an organization may not have a good idea as to who is in charge of making certain decisions. Whether we are trained to make certain decisions or not, all of us make many decisions every day of our lives.

Often people ask about decision-making skills. Two actions — making judgments and identifying possible alternatives — are involved in the decision-making process. Here is a road map in your decision-making process.

1. Identify the problem.
2. Analyze the situation and choose the best strategy.
3. Establish criteria or standards by which solutions will be evaluated.
4. Explore alternative solutions.
5. Select the most effective solution.
6. Implement the solution.

Strategies for Making Organizational Decisions

Management Decisions

What are the pros and cons?

Examples include decisions regarding the organization's policies or visionary goals made by management. The advantage of this strategy is that a decision can be made quickly to move the organization forward based on data at hand. Two disadvantages might be that you commit to a decision too quickly before pertinent data is available or you overlook valuable resources, including seeking feedback from your team.

Consultation Decisions

What are the pros and cons?

These are decisions where you get input from others, but the final decision is still made by you. Advantages of this strategy are that others in the organization may have valuable input and this contributes to the sense of teamwork. Disadvantages might be that you may not be able to use the input given. If you do not explain why you were not able to use their input, it may set a negative tone for future input.

Consensus Decisions

What are the pros and cons?

Decisions made after asking team members for input and only when everyone agrees to move forward are consensus decisions. Advantages of this strategy are that it creates teamwork and empowerment in the organization. The disadvantages are that it is the slowest strategy, and the best decision may be compromised.

Voting (Majority Decision)

What are the pros and cons?

One democratic way of making a quick decision is by a majority vote of the team. The disadvantage is that the minority may not accept and support the decision.

Decision-Making Styles

Team members should not only understand the various strategies utilized in the organization for decision-making process, but they should also be aware of the four styles of the leaders making the decisions.

- authoritative
- consultative
- facilitative
- delegative

The 80/20 Principle Applied to Job Search

Since the 80/20 Principle is the main focus of this book and my over-arching framework, I will simply highlight a few areas. This principle is apparent when your values conflict with institutional values more than 20 percent of the time, and you are in a discomfort zone. Remember, you are never going to find a 100 percent match in any organization, but most of us have certain values that we may not be willing to compromise. When we are not able to compromise, and we feel we cannot live with our conflicted conscience, then we may have to make a difficult choice and find an orga-nization that is a better fit.

It is crucial for the people who are going through a search process to understand their own guiding principles and to research the mission and values of the organization before accepting the position. It is equally important for an individual to ask about an organization's values during the interview processes, and in the same way, it is important for the orga-nization to understand the values of the individual.

As you go through the search process, if you believe that your values conflict with the organization's, particularly those values which are close to your core, then you may need to make a decision at an early stage and withdraw your application. Ninety-nine percent of people do not consider this when they are looking for a job; instead, people are focusing on simply finding a job. So, many times individuals are already sacrificing their own values to meet their personal priorities in life, such as daycare, housing, or personal finances.

As you go through the search process, sometimes you don't do enough research about the organization's values, and you don't ask the right ques-tions. Not doing so makes it difficult to turn down a position. Often, the consequences might be too great, so we shy away from doing the right thing for the right reason.

The 80/20 Principle Applied to Supervision

As a rule of thumb, my recommendation is that every person in an or-ganization should be empowered to make decisions for 80 percent of the items listed in their job description. If they don't have the respon-sibility to do this, I believe there will be a micro-management prob-lem in the organization. At times, some of the staff members may blame the organization's management for micro-management when they are unhappy with their supervisor or their position. Sometimes, there may not be a micro-management problem. It is important for every employee to review their job description and determine if they have the responsibility and ownership to make 80 percent of the decisions. Also, look at the type of decisions that are made beyond your departmental level.

This is how I used the 80/20 Principle. All my direct reports were trained annually on this principle with the expectation that they would prepare an agenda for each meeting. The following template, which describes percentage allocations and expectations, can serve as a guide for staff meetings when making decisions about priorities and task completion.

80 Percent

Since employees were expected to have decision-making responsibilities for 80 percent of their job description, this part of the meeting was informative, with an opportunity to highlight certain areas. A majority of staff listed such responsibilities as their last agenda item.

10 Percent

Ten percent of the decision-making process falls into the consultative discussion item category, where the employees explained the decisions they had made. Most employees knew what they wanted to do, but also wanted to make sure we were on the same page. If we disagreed, I guided them through the decision-making process. Often, this was a time to re-affirm the decisions already made and instill confidence in their decision-making ability. Almost always this 10 percent was finalized during one-on-one meetings.

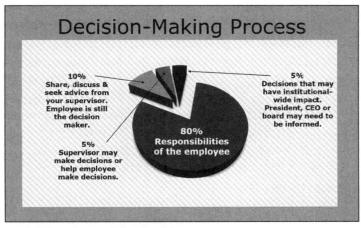

Model for the Decision-Making Process

5 Percent

Employees felt they needed guidance or that the decision was for me to make as the supervisor. Here again, the majority of the time, the decisions were made at this meeting. There can potentially be situations when additional time for research or further thought may be needed, but always provide a specific timeframe for this decision or response to be given to the employee. This particular section of the agenda was also an opportunity for coaching as well as some healthy give-and-take discussion.

5 Percent

The final part of the agenda constituted an institution-wide impact where the president of the institution or a CEO of an organization needed at least to be consulted so they were not blindsided about a situation. The items in the last 5 percent category were only occasional discussion items but nevertheless an important category.

If you follow this division of percentage as a template for the operation of your organization, chances are the decision-making process will occur as a seamless process within your organization, and employees will not have to wait for decisions to be made. If the 80/20 Principle is practiced at all levels within an organization, employees will be on the same page in terms of who and what decisions are made at what level, and it will eliminate the micromanaging complaint within an organization. Try it; you will like it. It works like magic.

Decision-Making: Terminating an Employee

Terminating an employee is one of the hardest decisions that you will make in your organization. As you review your hiring process and your employee performance process, are there challenges that could have been avoided through the hiring process? In some situations, you may not have been able to determine or avoid some of the issues. Sometimes, you have employees who just haven't developed a work ethic, and that can itself be a big challenge.

A poorly handled firing experience can undermine your confidence, make you look like a weak leader, and reflect badly on your organization. Authors Ken Blanchard and Spencer Johnson, in *The One Minute Manager*, identified some simple but very practical suggestions based on three principles: one-minute goal setting, one-minute praising, and one-minute reprimanding. Establish expectations through goal setting, provide opportunities for them to succeed, and give clear notice when there are problems.

How can you deal with possible deficiencies after an employee is hired? Maybe a better question might be why do you want to fire an employee? It is important that the management establish and provide specific standards and expectations in writing, and explain how the employee's actions are failing to meet those standards. When establishing expectations, they need to be specific and timely. It may be a good idea to have the goals, expectations, and the timeline co-signed by the employee and the supervisor, confirming he or she understands what is expected. The employee should also be forewarned of the consequences when expectations are not met. The employee should know if termination is a possibility.

Likewise, the human resources department should be consulted about all the steps that you are taking so that the process is fair, consistent, and legal. Follow all established procedures that include verbal and written warnings, probation, and termination. In addition, management must document every aspect of discussions and communications with your employee. Performance reviews should indicate goal achievements as well as areas for improvement. The infractions should be written down, dated, and kept in a secure file. If the employee does face termination, provide a detailed record to justify your decision soon after your face-to-face meeting with the employee. It is important to note that not all supervisors have the firing authority in certain organizations.

Advanced warning and clear documentation of an employee's conduct is not only a good management principle, but it also provides prudent legal protection. If termination is anticipated, having someone attend the meeting with you is always a good business practice. While it is a good idea to keep a formal record, it is also important to keep all aspects of your dealings with the employee professional, respectful, and ethical so that there is no gossip or e-mail about the employee's behavior or performance beyond your official documentation and discussions.

Depending on the basis for the termination, once fired, the employee should be required to leave the workplace as soon as possible. Make sure to secure all business documents, computers, keys, as well as take necessary and precautionary security measures.

Terminating an employee may be one of the hardest decisions that you make as a manager. It is also a process that to some extent the rest of the staff is observing, so the importance of handling the termination with utmost sensitivity and professionalism cannot be overstated. Your integrity and credibility as a leader are being closely observed.

Decision-Making: Good Process

An often-neglected but crucial ingredient in decision-making is a good process. A good process is a must in all aspects of the workings of an organization. Since we are talking about the decision-making process in this chapter, I cannot emphasize enough the importance of the role of a good process for an organization.

A cautionary tale is offered from one public institution that went through a major budget crisis due to a substantial reduction in the revenue for the state. Higher education funding was reduced significantly, so the institution was asked to cut its budget to the reduced level of funding and to come up with strategies to meet this goal. Those of you who are in higher education will attest to the fact that a budget cut of this magnitude is devastating, often resulting in cutting academic and co-curricular programs in addition to implementing furloughs, layoffs, and early retirements. At this institution, the president, several other administrators, and faculty senate followed a process to meet this mandate. Since personnel cost is the most significant component of most budgets, they had to accomplish this through early retirement and elimination of programs through which employees lost positions. All in all, several hundred positions were eliminated. Even though it was painful for all who were directly impacted, it all seemed manageable. Except there was one problem — lack of process in the reduction in workforce for some areas of the institution.

After leaders in some areas had worked hard to determine solutions to their portion of the institution's budget cut, a public and final decision was made by upper administration to preempt the process and instead to eliminate several administrators. This decision was clearly made without consultation and input from anyone within or affiliated with the unit.

It was not hard to understand the financial problems at hand. The institution was in a tough predicament to come up with millions of dollars through the budget reduction process in a short timeframe. The decision to reorganize may very well have been the right decision, but the problem here was a process that resulted in a loss of credibility among employees who even through this adversity demonstrated professionalism and character. The institution lost several other strong employees who felt that the institution had violated their values enough, tipping the scales of the 80/20 Principle, so that they could no longer work or succeed at the institution. What is the lesson here? We all may be put to the test in making some very tough decisions in our lives, including terminating employees, but we must never shortchange the process.

The Jennings Principle and Process

My former vice president, Dr. George Wallman, who is also my mentor, instilled in his employees the importance of process. I can say without hesitation he was a process-gatekeeper vice president. This is his legacy. His philosophy on process is engraved in the minds of those who were a part of his team.

His emphasis on process was developed over the years but was originally influenced by a course taught by Dr. Eugene E. Jennings at what is now the business college at Michigan State University. Jennings also wrote *Routes to the Executive Suite*. Chapters of his book covered aspects of good process, implementing an action plan, understanding opposition, and estimating how individuals, especially a leader, can act under stress.

Jennings processed the steps that are taken between the setting of a goal, the plan of action to achieve the goal, and the end result. The plan of action has several parts to it. The first is to gather information by listening to what others have to say and being willing to compromise. Hopefully, this results in a consensus of a final plan of action.

A lot of things happen as a leader presents an idea and listens to others for their response. One of the most common pitfalls is the stress a leader feels due to a lack of understanding of process opposition. This misunderstanding can result in taking all suggestions personally.

Understanding What Good Organizational Process Looks Like

First of all, we all need to be on the same page about organizational process, which takes place between setting your goal, your plan of action, and achieving your goal. The plan of action is just as important as the substance of the goal. You can have a great idea or vision, but without good process a leader may be unable to achieve consensus and buy-in.

Attributes of good organizational process include:

- Openness: Sometimes leaders feel strongly about an issue, so they are not willing to listen or to be open to other opinions. Allow yourself to hear other perspectives.

- Adequate time: Discussing a plan of action may involve too much or too little time. If a plan is pushed too fast, others in the discussion might react negatively. On the other hand, too much time might cause the plan to drag on. A leader needs to pay attention to how the plan of action is progressing, observing whether it is pushed too fast or it is bogged down in the process.

- Willingness to tune in to what others are saying: Listening is one thing, but along with it comes a need to understand what is being said. Understanding this is especially important in order to grasp the essence of any opposition. There are times when such opposition contains important insights.

- Willingness to compromise: Creating an environment for different opinions to be shared may have a significant value in an organizational process. This willingness may also improve the chances of others adopting the plan of action.

Anytime you are moving an idea forward, you should think about possible roadblocks ahead. Even if you are not faced with these problems, it is important to anticipate and understand some of the possible opposition. What are the types of opposition roadblocks a leader should expect?

1. Idea opposition: Even though you may get frustrated and disagree, if someone has a good rationale for opposing an idea, this may be beneficial if it provides clarity about the new idea being discussed.

2. Organizational process opposition: When individuals feel the plan is being pushed on them, especially without a broad enough context, they may push back. The leader may not pick up on this feeling and simply think the individuals do not like the plan when they are really reacting to how the idea is being presented or pushed forward. A good example is when a provost spent the summer redoing the class schedule to a point where the provost felt pretty good about it. Two weeks prior to the beginning of the fall quarter, the schedule was revealed to the faculty and student senate. There was immediate opposition and pushback. The provost was frustrated and personally hurt that others did not value all the time spent reorganizing the schedule. What really was going on was opposition to the provost's organizational process, which in reality was nothing more than an assumption that nobody else had to be consulted.

3. Personal Opposition: In an organization, someone sitting on a committee may be unhappy about something the leader said or decided in the past, or it may be that they just do not like them. Sometimes nothing can be done to satisfy that person. This is personal opposition, and it can be very difficult to overcome. Hopefully, in a group setting there is enough support for the leader's goal to overcome personal opposition.

Understanding opposition is important as a leader processes a plan of action toward a goal. Having a personal opponent can be difficult to change. There is always a possibility for compromise when faced with opposition to your goal. The combination of any of these types of opposition may be extremely difficult to overcome.

The bottom line is that you need to always anticipate opposition when moving forward with a process. Without being open-minded and willing to adapt the plan, a process cannot be successful. These are some possible scenarios while going through a process.

- Good idea/poor process usually leads to resistance to the idea.
- Poor idea/good process sometimes can result in support for a poor idea.
- Good idea/good process is the best of the possibilities.

Always keep in mind that most problems are related to poor process. Often, individuals and organizations get themselves into trouble not because of what they were trying to do, but the way they went about it. Usually, they have good ideas, good intentions, and good substance but fail in how they go about it.

Eugene Jennings's concept of process fit nicely into this approach. I utilized this concept numerous times in my professional and personal life and shared this concept with others at conferences and seminars. In fact, this concept may have been one of the most useful tools I learned and utilized in my professional career.

Factors Affecting Decision-Making . . . The Stress Cycle

The following terms illustrate some factors that affect decision-making and perceptions when we are involved in conflict resolution, disagreements, and difficult personal situations. The stress cycle can be brought on by personal opposition or the realization that you have a bad idea or process. It represents a leader losing confidence in their leadership.

Pre-Selecting Advice

All of us tend to pre-select our advice when we want to justify our own rationale or opinions. In these situations, we know exactly who to go to, and this person will tell you what you want to know and hear. The key word here is *want*, not what we need to hear. We all have these people in our lives who truly care about us but don't want to disappoint us, so they will always stay supportive. They are the feel-good people. We all need them, but they are not necessarily useful when we need to resolve a problem or a situation. Sometimes, the truth hurts, but it is crucial that we identify people who will always be truthful to you.

I had two people in my life who I often consulted, and both of their names happened to be Sandy. Sandy, my beloved wife, and my colleague Dr. Sandy Holbrook, who was the director of Equity and Diversity at NDSU, were the people that always told me what I needed to know and were always truthful. Their responses, particularly if they disagreed with my ideas and solutions, were not always immediately well received by me. This happened often with my wife. I knew I had the freedom to show my displeasure to my wife Sandy more freely than to my colleague Sandy. Without question, consulting these two people always was the right thing to do. I never regretted it.

Filtering Information

In stressful or conflicting situations, most of us are selective and hear only what we want to hear by filtering information. Most of the time, we are selective about hearing only the negative aspect of the conversation and filtering out the positive.

Magnifying Events

With conflict, we tend to magnify the situation and blow things out of proportion. We overreact to an event or situation and further contribute to the heightened emotional state or stress level. It is likely that if you were asked to summarize the account of the event, your version will be an altered, magnified version of the actual situation.

Focusing on Constraints

We often go through the stages described above and latch onto the negative, rationalizing our plight or dilemma. Our human tendency is to think about the negatives when we are in a stressful situation.

Misusing of Penalties

As a result of all stages that we may go through in conflict or a stressful situation, our tendency would be to treat the person involved unfairly or inappropriately depending on the situation. Because of these intense emotions, your tendency would be to make an example of this person by treating the person unfairly and in a punitive and harsh manner. In an educational environment, if you are the adjudicating officer involved in this situation, it is always advisable to remove yourself as the person responsible for assessing sanctions for the individual.

As a psychologist, Jennings had a keen understanding that stress was an emotional reaction that leaders had to be aware of and understand in order to be effective leaders.

Ethical Decision-Making

Now, let's talk about another principle in the decision-making process: ethical decision-making. Ken Blanchard and Norman Vincent Peale, co-authors of *The Power of Ethical Management*, suggest some simple guidelines to the question of what is an ethical decision:

- Is it doing what is right?
- Is it doing what is legal?
- Does it feel right?
- Would I feel embarrassed if the story appears in the newspaper?

The answer to the first question is deep-rooted in your response to all these questions. The decision-making process is complex, and at times there are situations that cloud our judgment. In the past, I have used three criteria adopted from Blanchard and Peale in evaluating decisions at all levels. In all situations, you need to give extensive and critical thought to your decisions and how they will impact you. Before moving forward with a decision, utilize these criteria to make your decisions.

Criteria 1: Right vs Wrong

Can you differentiate between what is right and what is wrong? All of us are compelled to evaluate right versus wrong. "Is it the right thing to do?" is a common query I have used throughout my career, something my father taught me at a very young age. We must always make decisions that are the right thing to do for ourselves and others. Is it fair to all concerned in the short and long-term? Does it promote a win-win situation?

Criteria 2: Legal vs Illegal

Most of us have a sense of what is legal and what is not legal. Will I be violating either civil law or company policy? Always follow all local, state, and federal laws.

Criteria 3: Do the right thing for the right reason.

As individuals, always seek to do the right thing for the right reasons. How would your decisions be perceived by the public, and would they hold up under public scrutiny? If the headline in your local newspaper is about the decision that you made, will it make you feel guilty, ashamed, or proud? Would I feel good if my family and friends knew about it? If your conscience is clear, you can feel good that you have made the right decision.

Criteria 4: God's Guidance

Let me give a fourth criteria, which is mine: God's Guidance.

For the past several decades, I have always brought God into the picture when making a tough decision. Previously, I used to bring God into my decision-making process after I had already resolved the problem, and then I simply asked for his blessing. If you truly want God's guidance, bring God in on the front end and seek His guidance. Such guidance often provides clarity in my decision-making process even if the decision may not have a positive outcome (or, an easy resolution). Where God comes into play in your decision-making process is entirely up to you. I have grown in my faith and my relationship with God, so I will not leave God out of my decision-making process.

The other day I was having a conversation with my son, and I told him that reaching a win-win situation in a difficult conflict by adhering to some of the principles cited above was the most intriguing, challenging, invigorating, and satisfying experience of my professional career. The bottom line is to always treat others the way you want to be treated — with fairness, respect, and dignity. I hope your experience will be the same. Have fun doing it!

5

WE ARE CALLED TO LEADERSHIP
...
TO DO THE RIGHT THING

As I completed my introductory chapter, one question stood out: what does *doing the right thing for the right reason* mean?

So, I selected several of my higher education friends and colleagues, whom I value very much, to seek their perspective and observations about the following scenarios based on their experience personally, professionally, and nationally:

- doing the right thing for the right reason,
- doing the right thing for the wrong reason, and
- doing the wrong thing for the right reason.

Before I share their feedback, let me share my own thoughts about how we all are challenged in our lives to make the right decisions.

For me, conscience plays an important role in our decision-making process. As I grew into my adulthood, I had many situations wrestling with my conscience. A person must work hard to follow their conscience or deal with the consequences. In chapter three, I talked about the three-cornered stone, illustrating how repeated wrongdoings have a cumulative and desensitizing effect on the conscience making it difficult to distinguish right from wrong. Benjamin Franklin composed this little rhyme: "Keep conscience clear, then never fear." Similarly, the great Irish writer George Bernard Shaw said, "Better keep yourself clean and bright; you are the window through which you must see the world." It seems like both of these people felt conscience is an important concept that will serve as the driving force for doing the right thing for the right reason.

I have been making an intentional effort in my life to do the right thing for the right reason. I learned that authenticity plays a role in demonstrating many aspects of life. None of us are perfect. We all have weaknesses and flaws. When we cover up our flaws and project an image inconsistent with who we really are, and at the same time are judgmental about other people's flaws, we are not practicing authenticity.

Another guiding force for doing the right thing is our motives. What motivates us to make the decision to move forward in doing the right thing or wrong thing? Where do those standards come from? Is it societal norms and standards? Your own moral compass? What happens when you encounter something different from your own values and standards? Do you take a stand to say this is not the right thing to do, and then you negotiate? What if no compromise can be reached? How do you know what to do and how to move forward in your decision-making process, or do you simply back off?

I believe rules and regulations are often made to do the right thing for the right reason, but if everyone did the right thing, there may not be a need for any rules. So, when we do the wrong thing for the right reason, it is because we are in disagreement with the rules that are established. I would add that if it is a life or death matter, it may be the right thing for the right reason.

I have worked very hard during the past four decades to model good behavior and practice doing the right thing for the right reason, particularly for my family. When I die, I want to be remembered for who I was as a person rather than for all my accomplishments. My integrity is of utmost importance to me. I would hope that the people with whom I worked and associated will remember me in this regard. My life has changed more spiritually in the last decade, giving God the number one priority. I used to be more concerned about how people viewed me. Image building was a high priority for me. There is nothing wrong with our desire to be accepted, appreciated, and approved by other people, but you cannot lead your life without God's approval. If you do this without giving the number one priority to God, your life will be built on a false image.

Now let me share with you a true story that you may ponder and decide as a case study. I traveled recently to India with my two adult sons and daughter-in-law. One of the goals of the trip was to introduce my daughter-in-law to our Indian family roots and travel across the country to educate her about Indian culture and customs. While in India, we took a boat ride from the city of Bombay to a site known as the Elaphanta Caves. As we entered the site, I noticed two lines for the tickets, one for Indian nationals and the other for foreign nationals. The Indian line was long, and the foreign line was short with one caveat: the Indian nationals' cost was forty rupees (about fifty cents), and the foreign nationals' cost was four hundred rupees (about five dollars). I was astounded! I knew I could afford this, but I was really unhappy with how they were justifying two standards for their visitors. I looked at the sign a few times and decided to stand in line and let them know my displeasure and use my negotiating skills to see if I could pay the lower rate.

When I got to the front of the line, they knew instantly I was standing in the wrong line, so they asked me if I was an Indian national. Well, I did not lie, but I did not answer their question directly either. Instead, I told them that I was born in India and lived in India for about two decades before I settled in the United States as a citizen. The woman at the ticket counter asked, "What about your family?" Again, I responded truthfully that they were born in the United States. Well, we argued for a while, and she gave in and gave me four tickets for forty rupees each. I felt like I was a great negotiator and victorious for about thirty seconds. All along my family was observing my bizarre and inappropriate behavior. As soon as I showed them my tickets, they let me know their displeasure. In fact, they let me know that I was simply wrong. I defended my stance by letting them know that I did not lie. But it was simply not acceptable to them, and they declared loud and clear, "You're beating the system, Dad."

We were having an amazing time up until this moment in our trip, but now I faced this tense moment with disappointment. Again, my instinct was to justify my behavior, but they didn't buy into it. The next step was to go through the ticket check post where I was scrutinized again and told that those tickets were meant for Indians living in the country. This time, I did not argue but restated that I was born in India and lived in India for about twenty years. Nevertheless, I was sent back to get four tickets for the foreign nationals for four hundred rupees each.

I felt strongly that my identity was questioned, and I needed to let them know this was not an acceptable practice. At the same time, I knew I violated the intent of their policy. I may not have lied, but I failed by trying to justify my birthright having been born in India. There was no excuse for what I did, and I felt ashamed. I profusely apologized to my family. Even after I got back from the vacation, this was still bothering me, so I had to apologize again in writing to my sons and daughter-in-law because my conscience clearly indicated that what I did was wrong.

To me, this was an example of doing the wrong thing for the right reason. I believed my reason for protesting unfair pricing practices was right, but my actions were not. I shared this experience with colleagues, and they all had a different viewpoint about my assessment and justification of my actions. Most of them defended me, even though I am still convinced I was wrong and in agreement with my children. What do you think?

Now let me share with you the feedback that I received from my colleagues in higher education regarding doing the right thing for the right reasons, doing the right thing for the wrong reasons, and doing the wrong thing for the right reasons. They each addressed their responses from their own perspective.

──────── • • • ────────

Dr. Gwen Dungy
Executive Director, Emeritus
NASPA-Student Affairs Administrators in Higher Education

In considering examples of doing the right or wrong thing for the right or wrong reasons, one must first wrestle with whose right thing is being considered. Additionally, it is important to understand how we each prioritize given values differently and how our own priorities might differ from those involved in any given decision.

As a career counselor, I took the Rokeach Value Survey. The survey includes thirty-six values; eighteen are instrumental values and eighteen are called terminal values. The terminal values are end result values such as a comfortable life or family security. The instrumental values, such as ambitious and logical, are how one would go about accomplishing one's terminal values.

Fifty years later, I can still recall that my top two terminal values were equally important to me. Forced to rank them, I chose freedom as my number one value and equality as my second value. Interestingly, I don't recall how I ranked my instrumental values or those values I would employ to eventually attain what I interpreted as freedom and equality. It probably does not come as a surprise that I, a Black woman in the United States fifty years ago, would rank freedom and equality high among my values.

I learned from my family and observations that education was the key to success, but as Black people we had to reach higher than others to retrieve the key. I have discovered through experience that all keys are not distributed equitably. Therefore, I will continue to work toward my values of freedom and equality and help others who have similar values whether explicit or not.

While not identified as values on the Rokeach Value Survey, I have discovered the instrumental values that have been my touchstones through the years. These values that have undergirded my sense of self and my way of interacting with others took form and became concrete when I have been asked questions about my career journey. People, especially younger people, are curious about how I as a Black woman who had to attend segregated schools in the South until after Brown vs Board of Education, and whose grandparents and mother were sharecroppers in the Mississippi Delta, could achieve the kind of success that I have attained.

As I continued to share anecdotes about my journey, I began to realize that there were consistent ways that I responded to day-to-day encounters and especially challenges. I had not named these ways of behaving until I reflected upon them through my journaling.

My journaling has been a constant companion as a way to record my history and to identify my feelings about events in my life. When I recorded as objectively as I could what was occurring in my day-to-day experiences and how I responded, I discovered consistencies that have become my instrumental values. A practice that has been essential to my emotional equilibrium has been to reflect daily on my experiences and subsequent feelings. Reflection has become a major instrumental value for me.

Other instrumental values come out of my history and experiences as well. When I hear about the childhood distress some have endured and compare their experiences to mine, I sometimes feel that my experiences cannot compare in severity. At these times, I recall homilies such as, "While I was complaining about not having any shoes, I saw a person who had no feet." Nevertheless, my childhood felt turbulent, unsafe, and relentlessly taxing.

Growing up without a consistent adult presence as a role model and protector, I cobbled together what I learned on those occasions when I went to the grand Methodist Church in Memphis or the humble storefront churches in Chicago. I took lessons from Sunday school for children, preachers' sermons, and, most of all, I learned and felt nourished by the songs we sang. I took the words to heart, and when there was no one to soothe, protect, or encourage me, I would recall lyrics from songs such as

"We Have Come This Far by Faith," "Have Thine Own Way Lord," "His Yoke Is Easy," "In the Garden," and "His Eye Is on the Sparrow." One summer in Bible school, we sang "Jesus Loves the Little Children." From the songs, I drew strength and comfort in the knowledge that Jesus's love was for all children, including me.

Though these lyrics are not always uppermost in my mind, the feelings evoked in me by the words and music remain. I have named this feeling of optimism based on my belief in a benevolent power faith.

My experiences and the accompanying lessons and admonitions taught me that I had to put forth more effort than people who are generally looked upon favorably because of some external feature or sheer chance or luck. Working harder and looking for opportunities to do more caused me to stand out and be noticed. In every position I've had, the job description changed because I expanded the responsibilities and increased the visibility of the work. I always looked for what more could be done and what could be done better or differently. This behavior earned me attention and respect. Fruits of my labor included being pushed forward to the next opportunity. My consistent behavior in my work was what I see as an instrumental value that I call initiative.

When I was growing up, a common and frequent admonition was that I should not be so sensitive. It seemed that people could hurt my feelings more easily than they could hurt others. Often, I would be told to say, "Sticks and stones may break my bones, but words will never hurt me." But the words did—and still do—hurt me. Not only do I continue to feel emotional pain from words, I feel pain for others who are treated harshly, suffer a loss, or need help that I might be able to provide. I continue to have a keen sense of others' feelings, and when I sense that they need someone to hear them, feel with them, or help them, I always want to be one of the first to step forward. Whether a colleague or the designated leader, I remain sensitive to the feelings and needs of others. I value this in myself and name this value empathy.

These values have helped steer decisions I have made in my life and career. When making these decisions, I've always been motivated by doing the right thing.

One instance that stands out for me in determining whose right thing is being considered was when I was an academic dean and I knowingly made a decision that was against fiscal policies for the institution. I was aware that, if I were called on the decision, it could have had devastating consequences for me. Yet, I made the decision because I thought that the outcome would be worth the risk.

I did the wrong thing according to policies. However, I did not compromise my moral beliefs and values. No one was hurt by my decision. I made a serious infraction of the rules. I had requested an exception and flexibility on the rules to no avail. If I had not violated the policy, faculty and students would have missed an opportunity that they had worked toward in good faith. I had empathy for them and faith that the consequences would not cost me too dearly. If I had not shown initiative in taking what was a drastic action, the positive outcomes would not have been possible. I reflected on my decision and actions at length, and did not waiver in my conviction that, although I did the wrong thing according to policy, I did the right thing for the largest number of people.

———— • • • ————

Dr. Laura Oster-Aaland
Vice Provost for Student Affairs and Enrollment Management
North Dakota State University

I am fortunate to have worked for ethical leaders throughout my career. These leaders led by example, examining their own biases and assumptions as they processed the difficult decisions before them. One leader emphasized the process that was used for decision-making. He placed great value in assuring that all stakeholders in a decision were invited to the table to discuss, debate, and to be heard. Through this process of discernment, he asked hard questions, required evidence, and considered impacts on all parties. In the end, a decision was made, and a rationale provided. The process played out and we trusted that the outcome was sound. We learned to trust the process.

Another great leader empowered and affirmed her direct reports. She created a safe space for testing out our decisions — she gently guided and directed us when we were off course and enthusiastically affirmed us when we succeeded. Her values put people in the center as she artfully found ways to strike compromise while continuing to move forward. Her empathy resulted in humane decisions, and even when some disagreed, they could not fault her motives. We learned to trust in her, in one another, and in ourselves.

Another ethical leader was firmly grounded in a strong sense of right and wrong. His decision-making was based on a generational understanding of ethics passed down from his parents, particularly his father. His guiding mantra, "Do the right thing for the right reason," was his measuring stick for himself and those of us who reported to him. His honesty with himself and others made us strive to be our best selves in both the professional and personal sense. He used a combination of head and heart in his decision-making. His process was measured, careful, and thorough. We learned self-examination of our actions and our motives.

As I reflect on the decision-making of my three mentors, I am struck by how often they got it right. Rarely were their decisions questioned by their peers or direct reports. While they may have each employed different tactics, they seemed to reach the same result — that is, they "did the right thing for the right reason." I am challenged and honored by the request of my friend and mentor, Prakash Mathew, to answer the following three questions as they relate to making ethical decisions. What does it mean to 1) do the right thing for the right reason, 2) do the right thing for the wrong reason, and 3) do the wrong thing for the right reason?

As I reflect on the three questions, I think about what it means to understand right and wrong. Is the right thing always clear? Is right and wrong an objective truth or is it contextual, based on the circumstances we encounter? And how do we examine our reasons for taking a course of action? Are our reasons always clear to us? It seems that doing the right thing for the right reason requires a framework to determine what is right and a self-awareness to determine our motivations.

What does it mean to do the right thing for the right reason?

Doing the right thing for the right reason feels like alignment. Alignment happens when my values about what is right in a certain situation align with my motivation for taking a certain action. What is the framework that helps me determine what is right? My framework comes from a combination of my upbringing and my life experiences. An early memory includes running errands with my mother when I was about four years old. Running errands was not my favorite activity. I enjoyed being with my mom, but I was bored by the endless waiting as it seemed at every stop she had to visit with the people in the store. She often said, "This will just take a minute," and I knew that meant it would take a long time. During one of these errand runs, I was eyeing the candy counter at the drug store where we had stopped. I badly wanted a piece of licorice, and so I simply reached over and took one. My mother paid her bill, and we left the store. While in the car, I took out my licorice and began to enjoy it. Of course, my mother asked where I got the licorice and I said I took it. On some level, I knew that what I did was wrong, but my mother's reaction confirmed it. She took the licorice away and told me I would have to go back to the store, apologize, and pay for it.

I think many of us share a similar story from our childhoods as we learn to control our impulses and respect the rules of ownership. The fact that I remember this story as an adult tells me that it shaped me in a profound way. It was not only the foundation of learning right and wrong, it taught me how to own my mistakes and seek forgiveness and reconciliation. The principles learned in this simple childhood story confirm for me that right and wrong is something we learn and something that takes practice. What would have happened if my mother had not made me apologize? I'm sure I would not have grown up to be a candy thief; however, an upbringing of consistent parental guidance has surely resulted in values that help discern right from wrong.

My mother died of cancer when I was six years old. I have few memories of my mother, but the memories that I have are happy. My mother was a nurse. She was a busy professional at a time when not many moms worked outside the home. I have memories of adventures with various babysitters and caregivers. I also have memories of my mom in her nursing uniform bringing us toys from work and her caring for me when I was sick. She was joyful and attentive. Many years later when I became a mother, I struggled with guilt after returning to work. I loved my job as a mid-level student affairs professional, but I struggled to know if working was the right thing to do. And I questioned my motives. I felt guilty for enjoying my job and sad to leave my baby with a caregiver, but honestly, I felt a sense of relief being able to be just me for eight hours a day.

When I shared my conflicted feelings with my father, he told me how my mother decided to stay home after each of her three children were born. She loved her job as a nurse, but after her babies came, she felt she should stay home and be a full-time mom. He told me that she made it six months with each of us. Each time, she would become unhappy, unfulfilled, and grouchy (as my dad described it). He told her she needed her work. It was an important part of her identity and that she could still be a loving and committed mother if she worked full-time. And so she did.

This story took a weight off my shoulders and helped me examine my reasons for my decision to be a mother and to work full-time. I was doing the right thing for me for the right reasons. My memories of my mother were nothing but positive and her working did not detract from those memories. When I examined my motivations, I realized that they were aligned with my decision. I wanted to be a mom — it was an important part of my identity — and I wanted to contribute professionally. When our values align with our motivations, we are doing the right thing for the right reason. Doing the right thing for the right reason leads to a sense of satisfaction and resolve.

What does it mean to do the right thing for the wrong reason?

This question is the most difficult of the three. It speaks to our motivations. Sometimes we do the right thing for personal attention or recognition. And sometimes we do the right thing to cover ourselves for how it might look to others. As a parent, we can see our young children practice this behavior. As we are teaching them to resist their impulses and temptations, they will often comply with our wishes so that they can get a reward. For instance, please stop hitting your brother or you will need to take a time out. You can have a cookie if you eat your vegetables. These types of bargains are often necessary parenting tools; however, they provide external motivation that is unrelated to the behavior at hand. The child's motivation for doing the right thing is based on avoiding consequence or achieving reward. This is appropriate in the teaching of children, but if relied upon as our only benchmark for decision-making into adulthood it can be problematic.

Another example that comes to mind is my personal struggle with healthy eating and exercise. I struggle to maintain consistency with both goals. Often in the spring, I make a commitment to get myself to the gym so that I can tone my body for summer. What is my motivation for this? I'd like to look better in my summer clothes! Ultimately, I am not likely to keep my commitment to my health goals because I am motivated by the wrong thing — external motivation. Motivation that is lasting comes intrinsically from within. When I commit to healthy eating and exercise because I want to feel good and maintain a good quality of life for myself and my family, I am more likely able to sustain my practices.

Doing the right thing for the wrong reason is often difficult to discern in oneself and requires significant self-reflection. There are times when the right thing is so important that our reason really doesn't matter — it's simply the correct course of action. Other times, when we are seeking attention, recognition, or simply avoiding a negative consequence, the right thing may be diminished by our motivation.

What does it mean to do the wrong thing for the right reason?

Doing the wrong thing for the right reason is justified when policies conflict with values or when an exception needs to be made to accomplish a greater good. I think of civil disobedience of unjust laws or public protest to raise consciousness. These actions may violate law or policy, but they raise consciousness of a greater good. Of course, there is subjectivity to determining if an action is truly wrong and if a reason is inherently right. The recent controversy over professional athletes kneeling during the national anthem is a case in point. Other examples stand the test of time and become more universally accepted, such as the sit-ins at the lunch counters during the civil rights protests of the 1960s or Rosa Parks taking a seat at the front of the bus and starting the Montgomery bus boycott.

Most of us would agree that honesty is one of the most important values and being transparent professionally is important. Yet there are times when a supervisor shares information with us that cannot be shared with others because it would damage the reputation of another individual or the institution. Sometimes this puts us in a situation where we are less than forthcoming with our peers or colleagues and makes us feel compromised. This is technically doing the wrong thing (withholding information) yet for the right reason (to protect an individual or the institution's reputation).

Doing the wrong thing for the right reason requires a firm commitment to one's values and sometimes carries consequence. Professionally, it is sound practice to seek feedback and counsel from trusted colleagues — to check our assumptions. Several examples come to mind where I have needed to make an exception to a policy to achieve the best outcome for a student. Admitting a student who does not meet admission requirements, but who has overcome personal barriers in her life which show promise, is an example of doing the wrong thing for the right reason.

There is a growing practice in higher education of providing "micro-grants" for students who have outstanding balances of $2,500 or less and are in their last year of school. Typical practice is to put a hold on students' accounts to not allow registration. This can lead to delayed graduation as students are not able to register for needed classes as well as dropping out altogether. Certainly, most students can pay their bills and should be held accountable to do so. However, some students simply have access to fewer resources and after careful scrutiny could benefit from an act of grace such as a micro-grant to pay off their balance so they can complete their education. Institutions who have embraced this practice have significantly increased their graduation rates, especially for under-represented students. Additionally, these institutions have found that the revenue generated by keeping the student in school compensates for the expense of these targeted grants. This is an example of doing the wrong thing for the right reason — bending a policy for the greater good.

Ultimately, doing the right thing for the right reason is a helpful mantra for us to live honest, authentic lives and to be successful professionals. Using this standard to measure our decisions requires self-reflection, careful discernment, and sometimes the feedback of trusted colleagues and friends. Sound decision-making requires a healthy mix of thinking and feeling. When I am at peace with my decisions in both my head and my heart, I can usually know that I got it right.

——— • • • ———

Dr. Diana Doyle

President of Arapahoe Community College
Littleton, Colorado

Doing the Right Thing for the Wrong Reason:
We make it about helping people.

I believe that people are basically good. Most of us, especially leaders in education, want to help people, do right by them. This may lead to our making a decision we think is the right thing to do — but in actuality is the wrong thing — because we believe our reason for doing so is to help someone. Unfortunately, our good deed may come back to bite or haunt us (the old adage of "no good deed goes unpunished"). When a student or employee asks for special allowance, exception, or treatment, our first inclination usually is to consider it — take it on an individual case basis. Often when students or employees make these requests, it's not about righting a wrong or needing to address an equity issue. It is about their wanting something to go their way to meet their need. Student affairs professionals are trained and educated to be helpers who want to see people succeed. It's tempting to just give the person what they're asking for, especially if they keep pushing. We convince ourselves that we are doing right by this person. In these situations, we need to ask ourselves if we are making a precedent-setting decision to exempt a student or employee from a policy, procedure, or requirement. In the short run it may resolve an issue for that person (or get them off our back), but in the long run it opens the door for others wanting or expecting the same exception or special treatment. While our intentions were good — sincerely wanting to help someone — the ultimate result often does not help their personal growth and only perpetuates their belief that they are above the policies, rules don't apply to them, or that they are more deserving than others. This also may leave a negative impression for other students or employees who follow the rules and cast the Student affairs professional in a negative light. Are there exceptions to this? Absolutely! Educational leaders must always weigh the factors for doing the right thing and be honest about their reasons for doing so.

Doing the Wrong Thing for the Wrong Reason: We make it about us.

Saying yes to the student or employee request for special exception, allowance, or treatment is appealing, especially for less experienced leaders, because no one wants to be seen as not having compassion or not being a caring person interested in an individual's situation. In this instance, we take the focus off of the student or employee—where it should be—and instead make it about us and our feelings. Experience and lessons learned when our decision comes back to haunt us help us understand that it's not about us. The focus should remain on the student or employee.

Doing the Right Thing for the Right Reason: We make it about learning and respect.

Even though it may seem counter-intuitive, sometimes the hardest decision as a leader is to do the right thing for the right reason. Denying the student or employee request for special treatment may be difficult, but seeking a resolution that sustains both sides of the request keeps the greater good in mind. More importantly, we leaders have an opportunity to positively impact an individual's personal growth and development (whether they see it that way or not) and take the teachable moment to demonstrate respect for all students and employees. Having a positive impact on others' growth and development—isn't that one of the reasons why we became leaders in the first place?

——— • • • ———

Dr. Bruce Maylath

Professor of English

North Dakota State University

- *Doing the right thing for the right reason*
- *Doing the right thing for the wrong reason*
- *Doing the wrong thing for the right reason*

Since first viewing this list of actions and reasons, I've found myself dwelling repeatedly on the second one, "Doing the right thing for the wrong reason," in particular because I read them just after viewing the premiere of the documentary *The Mission of Herman Stern*. The film gives attention not only to North Dakota businessman and Jewish immigrant Herman Stern, who did the right thing for the right reason in helping over 140 family members and friends escape Nazi Germany and immigrate to the United States, but also devotes considerable attention to North Dakota US Senator Gerald Nye, who helped Mr. Stern behind the scenes to secure the State Department's clearance in approving immigration applications at a time when the United States was reluctant to admit more Jews. The irony is that, publicly, Senator Nye was outspoken in his anti-Semitism and voted accordingly in the Senate.

Senator Nye did the right thing in helping Mr. Stern and the specific Jewish refugees whom Mr. Stern helped to flee from the regime of Adolph Hitler and the Schutzstaffel. Why did he do the right thing for these Jews but the wrong thing for those not connected to Mr. Stern? We'll never really know what was going through the senator's mind—and heart. Was he simply interested in helping constituent Herman Stern, an earlier immigrant who was, by the 1930s, a highly influential community leader, not only in his town of Valley City but across North Dakota? Did he simply wish to curry Mr. Stern's favor? If so, we could say that, at least for these 140-plus Jews, the senator did the right thing but not to the full extent of right reasons. Sadly, in public, he did the wrong thing for the wrong reasons when it came to opportunities to help other Jewish refugees, so many of whom would go on to die in the gas chambers of the Third Reich.

In some respects, Senator Nye reminds me of the pharaoh who eventually allowed the Israelites to flee Egypt. The pharaoh did the right thing but for the wrong reason: namely, to try to avoid another plague, after already suffering seven. Even then, he tried to reverse himself when the Israelites reached the Sea of Reeds. The circumstances surrounding Senator Nye seem more complicated. Nevertheless, we can see in hindsight that he could and should have made the simple choice: to do the right thing for the right reason. Current and future senators would do well to learn how history now views Senator Nye.

While the rest of us may not be senators — much less pharaohs — all of us confront choices that demand that we do the right thing. It behooves all of us to consider whether we want our descendants to see that we did so for the right reasons.

——————— • • • ———————

Dr. George Wallman
Vice President for Student Affairs, Emeritus
North Dakota State University

As I write this, it is around the time of Senator John McCain's funeral. Numerous individuals have referred to McCain as having "done the right thing." Similarly, a PBS program by Ken Burns about the Mayo Clinic in Rochester, Minnesota, credited the Mayo brothers' success to "doing the right thing." Hardly a week goes by without someone in the news referring to someone as "doing the right thing." So, what does this phrase mean?

In an article from the Institute for Ethical Leadership, Desmond Berghofer addresses this question in the context of leadership. He says to do the right thing means to make a choice among possibilities in favor of something the collective wisdom of humanity knows to be the way to act. "To 'do things right' carries the meaning of efficiency, effectiveness, expertise and the like . . . [and] that a leader must call upon a broad band of intuitive knowledge and use it to give guidance and direction." Berghofer goes on to point out that we believe that somehow out of all the "myriad of possibilities in a complex world there is something we can call right action in a given situation," and we believe a leader will be able to find the "right thing and choose to do it, no matter what."[4]

To me, Berghofer is writing about the decision-making process, which is part of the leader's unique knowledge and value base, and that others are willing to follow.

---

[4] Desmond Berghofer, "Institute for ethical leadership. Doing the right thing." http://www.ethicalleadership.com/DoingRightThing.htm.

Doing the Wrong Thing for the Right Reason

During my first few months as vice president for Student Affairs at North Dakota State University, I showed up at a Student Senate meeting and stood in front of them asking for support to establish a new student fee for a new health center. I could tell from the non-verbal shifting in their seats, to looking at each other with something less than enthusiasm and something more than just confusion, that I was making a huge mistake. It was unanimously voted it down, and there I was, wondering why I was even there. After the senate meeting, a couple of students approached me about this, followed by several individuals coming to my office and explaining what happened in the meeting and making suggestions on how to approach this. They said that the senators were completely blindsided by my request and added that the need for a health center should be broadened to include a wellness concept. They were majoring in the Health Sciences field. What they said made sense and turned out to be a major influence on the remaining fifteen years of my vice presidency. The students helped me become aware of how wrong my process was even though there was a great need for a new health center. They created awareness in me that I had left them out of the process, and by doing so I did not benefit from their input. I decided, with the consultation of my cabinet, that this project needed to be turned over to the students' leadership for their input and for them to trust me in respecting what they would recommend. Some individuals were concerned that they would not support a new fee for a building. My response was, "That is their choice, not ours."

Students formed a Health and Wellness Task Force, visited other campuses, and brought experts to NDSU. They held informational meetings across campus, meeting with thousands of students to discuss their ideas and encourage input. My office provided the funds. It went to a vote of the entire student population and passed. The end result was a new Health and Wellness Center with an educational component. It was so successful that after one year, plans were developed for an addition.

But that isn't all. Those students caused me to encourage our directors to create student advisory groups that would become a hallmark of our work for years to come. So, doing the wrong thing for the right reason provided an opportunity for me to learn.

Doing the Right Thing for the Right Reason

I received a phone call while my wife and I were out eating. The voice on the other end of the phone was agitated trying to explain that there was a major fire on campus in one of our upper-class apartments. We immediately drove to the campus where the fire was raging. The fire destroyed a building housing about seventy-five students. Nobody was physically hurt, but it was obvious in talking to affected students that there was an emotional toll. They were fortunate to be alive. The next day in a meeting with our Residence Life leadership, I suggested that we refund the student's fees for housing for the entire quarter and not charge them anything for the next quarter as well. There was immediate consensus that this was the right thing to do. I gave the go ahead to proceed. The vice president for Finance disagreed; however, since the residence halls were in Student Affairs and he had no direct responsibility in this area, the president was also in agreement. It was the right thing to do for several reasons: we could afford it and I, along with the other leaders in that area, felt strongly that it was right to do given the emotion, stress, and sense of danger our students felt. Months later, feedback arrived from students and some parents of how grateful they were and how it had developed a very positive image of NDSU.

We were motivated by the right reasons to do the right thing.

———— • • • ————

Dr. Kate Haugen
Retired, Associate Vice President for Student Affairs
North Dakota State University

In reflecting on the questions of doing the right or wrong things for the right or wrong reasons, I have pondered, as have others, the difficulty in determining if right and wrong are purely black and white. Understandably, most would agree that variations of right and wrong exist in every person, determined by individual values, culture, history, and life experiences. We can struggle with the boundaries of right and wrong when considering what factors influence the decisions we make. Justification for our actions can be stretched in many directions with divergent reasoning.

As a young child, I learned early on that gaining the approval of others was a satisfying result. It fueled my lifelong uncertainty about not being good enough. And so, frequently, I turned outward for affirmation. Complicating this trait was my need for perfection — everything needed to be ordered and correct. I was always striving to do the right thing, but for right or wrong reasons? My parents were loving and not overly demanding. But there was no question about their expectations of me and my siblings to do our best and to work to become good and productive persons. Of course, I manifested these expectations into believing my best was not enough. This addiction to perfection created detours to living fully and completely and put unnecessary hurdles in the way. Thus, my discernments of right and wrong were colored by my own personality traits. I feel this is the case for each individual and his or her own characteristics that impact and filter their perception of right and wrong.

As I look back on my path through school, college, graduate work, and embarking upon a career, I realize how achievement and accomplishment became incentives each step of the way. While this reward system is not all bad, was it the right way to build a foundation that would contribute to a personal and professional life which was genuine, productive, fulfilling, and value-based?

With this background in mind, I explore some right and wrong issues in my professional and personal life from three perspectives.

Politics

Politics is a word with meanings that can be descriptive and non-judgmental. It can also carry a negative connotation. Most work settings have some degree of a political influence, typically hierarchical in nature. In higher education, the administrative structure and seniority system for faculty lends to the political environment at a college or university and shapes the governance of the institution. Functioning within this organizational realm can be challenging since its rules and regulations can at times be in conflict with the goals and values of its members.

The beauty of academic freedom is the ability, ideally, to discuss freely and openly issues and differences in a safe context. But in reality, there are sometimes dissensions which fester and can present obstacles to achieving desirable outcomes. This situation can lead to "working the system" or "playing politics" in order to maintain job security, protection of staff, and student advocacy. These circumstances may result in doing the right thing for the wrong reason merely for survival. Is this compromise worth the outcome?

Frequently, another attribute of politics in a system is the effort to achieve or use power.

Power

Power connotes control. In a work setting it, like politics, is typically a part of the hierarchy of the governance structure. It can be assumed due to position, but it can also be earned through leadership in achieving outcomes which benefit the common good — we see this often in student initiatives, faculty research, and administrative strategies.

Adam Grant, an organizational psychologist at Wharton School of Business, the University of Pennsylvania, asserts that in order to predict how people will use power, you need to figure out what their motives, values, and identities are before they have it. Are they generous givers or selfish takers? How you use authority reveals your character: selfish leaders hoard power for personal gain — the wrong thing for the wrong reason. Servant leaders share power for the social good — the right thing for the right reason. Grant also states that the ultimate test of character for people in power is how they treat people who lack it. This, too, aligns with doing the right thing for the right reason.

Power can bestow privilege, be it overt or inherent. I feel strongly that we must acknowledge and admit to both the positive as well as insidious impacts of privilege. Having been involved for many years of my career in college admissions, I am reminded of the privilege I was granted to make judgments and decisions that greatly affected all the student applicants. Following the admission standards was for the most part the normal path for reviewing applications — doing the right thing for the right reason. However, often a student presented circumstances that warranted more flexibility in interpreting those standards: a solid high school transcript but a difficulty taking standardized tests, major adversity in their personal lives, financial barriers, etc. These students might be evaluated with a bit of a bend to the standards — doing the wrong thing for the right reason?

And, of course, the recent admissions scandal of bribery by the wealthy to obtain admission to elite colleges is reprehensible. In addition, it reveals deeper and systemic issues with the attainability and affordability of higher education across the board. The wrong thing for the wrong reason.

Purpose

Whether a calling, a drive, or a life goal, finding purpose in what we do is aspirational. In my work in higher education, I held fast to the importance of consensus building, creating trust, caring that work was meaningful for staff, and that we all had valuable contributions to make. I adhered to a leadership model of transforming communities, which embraces interrelated responsibilities and rewards for all members of a community. In my case, the community consisted of my various staffing groups. This process is built on the premise that all members of the office community have responsibility, authority, and power, and that it is the responsibility of each to use it appropriately and to the benefit of the total organization. It embraces change as positive and growth-producing. Response to change, which is ongoing in any community, is vital to how the group moves forward.

One memorable change transition was the move to a new computer software system. The time and energy demanded of the staff to implement the system while continuing to maintain daily workflow were at times overwhelming. As many who have been through this process know, it takes a toll on the entire campus. And yet the effort to effect positive change was held as our primary goal.

At various points in the transition, many had difficulty believing we were doing the right thing for the right reason. As can happen in a bureaucratic mandate such as this, staff efforts did not always appear to be supported or appreciated universally. Ongoing encouragement to keep the bigger picture in mind was paramount to remembering our purpose and finding a successful conclusion to the project.

In my personal life, a part of my purpose was to be a loving mother and supportive role model to my son. As I mentioned earlier, I often was striving to do things for the approval of others. That meant following the rules, coloring inside the lines, and conforming to the accepted norms! But, as fate would have it, I found that my son did not adhere to those same ideas. His very creative, artistic, and independent nature took him down different paths and his actions, to me, were the wrong things for the wrong reasons. But his rebellious actions were also an eye-opening opportunity to step outside my box and see things through a different lens and from a new perspective, and to appreciate learning from him. What a gift it was to be schooled by my own child when I finally allowed myself to acknowledge and embrace his free spirit! In the end, perhaps the right things for the right reasons.

6

TO CREATE A CULTURE

This chapter is all about creating a culture for your organization. So how do you define culture? Culture is the mindset of an organization. Culture is the shared beliefs, norms, and values of a group of people. It is an expression of the way to do things in an organization. It also spells out how people are to behave.

Sometimes culture is a way of life in an organization. In today's social media and technology culture, we all need to get used to working in different cultures. I remember when I started my professional work, the culture of our organization was such that only a few members of the team knew how to use technology in the workplace. When we were making advancements in computer technology, some people in certain positions were given a computer with no expectation to use them. For about a year or so, I was still seeking assistance from our front office staff, and the computer stayed on my desk as a paperweight. Soon after this, I moved to another university, and the staff in this environment were knowledgeable about using computer technology in their daily work without depending on their support staff. Naturally, this new work environment put tremendous pressure on me to transition into this culture. First of all, I wanted to survive, and second, I did not want to be embarrassed about my incompetency. To overcome these two factors, I brought my wife to the workplace at night to teach me to be adequately competent in my new work environment and culture.

If everyone understands the culture of the workplace and reasons behind the culture, most people will buy into it, provided it is modeled by their CEO or the administration. It is important that there is a buy-in by the members of the organization about how people are supposed to do things and why guidelines are necessary. Some of the principles involved in instituting an organizational change process (which will be covered in chapter seven) can be beneficial to the buy-in process. Creating a culture where staff can speak openly and honestly without fear promotes a healthy and productive organization.

We often talk about the *buy-in* principle as part of the culture and a good rule of thumb before you implement a decision. So, how do you get buy-in from people? First, people need to know about your ideas, your game plan, and your rationale as to how this will be effective for the organization and the people whom you are serving. When soliciting feedback, are you open to their suggestions and ideas and willing to modify your proposal if necessary? If all parties involved are feeling good about the idea fully, it is likely that you have buy-in.

This does not mean that every idea you are initiating will go through without scrutiny and a lengthy buy-in process. To avoid delay, staff must know that there are certain decisions made by leadership at many levels that may not involve staff participation and input. One drawback to the buy-in concept is that it may take a longer period to make decisions. It would be a good practice for organizations to understand which types of decisions are made at different levels and which types of decisions may go through a buy-in process.

Some leaders in certain organizations practice an open-door policy. This policy is one way to demonstrate the culture of the organization. In other words, leaders are communicating openness to outsiders and the members of the organization that they welcome visits and feedback. I had an open-door policy; the staff knew that if my door was open, I was available for interruptions in my schedule. When I was in a meeting or doing work that required 100 percent concentration and privacy, I kept my door shut.

In most companies and organizations, leadership has its own ideas and plans as to how and to what direction the organization should move forward. Often, leaders implement their plans or chart their course of action without seeking any input from staff within the organization.

To use a planting metaphor—since flower gardening is my hobby—leadership is preparing the ground and planting the seeds. For seeds to germinate and flourish, preparation for planting—turning the soil, adding nutrients—is important. Likewise, inviting participation from people is important to shaping the culture of an organization and setting the vision.

Some leaders may be fearful of losing control of the organization's identity, but instead they maintain credibility for their organization by establishing certain boundaries and adhering to the core values of the organization, while welcoming team participation and input.

Mirror, Window, and Lantern Exercise

How do you describe the culture of your organization? In my Student affairs work, I used to do the mirror, window, and lantern exercise — developed by qualitative researcher Gary D. Shank — to get an idea about the culture of an organization.[5] Most of the time people do not have any idea how their organization is perceived by others or even by their own team members. Let me explain how I used the mirror, window, and lantern exercise.

Why do we look in the mirror? The mirror allows us to see and correct things we ordinarily cannot see in ourselves, and at the same time, shows flaws that others can see more easily. As a member or a leader of an organization, when you look in the mirror, what do you see? The mirror will reveal your flaws as well as ideas for improvement.

How about the windows? The window provides transparency and a clear and undistorted view. Is there anything that keeps our window from being transparent? When the window is smudged, we cannot see the true view. When others see us through the window, how do they perceive us? What do they see? If they were to describe your organization based on their view, how would they describe it? You are projecting an image about your organization. Can everyone see what you want them to see?

Jim Collins, author of *Good to Great: Why Some Companies Make the Leap and Others Don't*, observes that a leader with a humble heart looks out the window to find and applaud the true causes of success and looks in the mirror to find and accept responsibility for failure. The question then is how do you behave when no one is watching you?

Finally, let's take a look at the lantern. A lantern provides illumination, enlightenment, and insight. Our understanding of meaning is not complete until we discover and understand its role in practice and experience. How are we enlightened? What insight is gained when we see the world through the eyes of others? When the lantern illuminates, what is revealed as our strengths and weaknesses?

---

5 Gary D. Shank provided insight about this concept in *Qualitative Research: A Personal Skills Approach*, 2nd Ed. (2005).

Every business or organization has a culture. Sometimes that culture is fragmented and difficult to read from the outside. Shared values play an important role in communicating to the outside world what is expected of an organization.

Psychologist Angela Duckworth, in *Grit: The Power of Passion and Perseverance*, writes about Anson Dorrance, the women's soccer coach at University of North Carolina at Chapel Hill who won twenty-two national championships in thirty-one years. Dorrance was asked about the secret of his success. Without hesitation, he talked about the culture of his team, as well as everyone's understanding of the culture. This is how he responded: "We are out recruited . . . on a regular basis. Our extraordinary success is about what we do once the players get here. It's our culture."[6]

I witnessed such an effect based on culture at North Dakota State University with the football program. North Dakota State University won eight national championships in nine years in Division 1 FCS football. Past coaches and former head coach Chris Klieman will tell you this is who we are at North Dakota State. It is our Bison tradition and culture. They will also say that we are part of a family. Some institutions talk about similar principles and concepts, but is it part of their culture? If you have a culture that is solid in philosophy and practice, it can provide a model for others. When you adopt a culture, you also make allegiance to that team. This is how they demonstrate living their values.

Recently, I read an article written by my good friend, Marci Narum, co-editor of *Inspired Woman Magazine*. The article, "The Secret Sauce for Any Champion," is based upon her interview with former NDSU head coach Chris Klieman and focuses on the secret of the team's success. Instantly, Klieman proclaimed: "It's all about culture." He went on to describe the ingredients of the Bison football program's "Secret Sauce" culture in the following excerpts from Narum's article:

Show them you care:

- **Everything that we are doing within our football program is what a business is trying to do for their employee; a parent is trying to do for their child.**

- **What people see on the field is a great product. What I see off the field is a better product. For us, it is the whole person and the ability for the young man to get a great degree, to be able to play great football, but more importantly, to become a man.**

---

[6] Angela Duckworth, *Grit: The Power and Passion of Perseverance* (Scribner Book Company, 2016), p. 255.

Success is not measured by touchdowns and tackles or even championships. It starts with relationships. Trust and team building.

- Show them that you care. They play for each other for sure. They play for coaches that care, too. You need to show it's more than a game. You have to care for them on and off the field.

Attack Adversity:

- Attack adversity, not the players after a loss. Nobody ever raises a voice in the locker room. Nobody is critical of the guys' effort or how they played. Those guys are hurting anyway.
- The losses and hard times will always happen; how you respond in those moments is more valuable.
- Adversity brings out the best in a lot of people. Mediocre programs are destroyed by it, good programs survive it, and great programs and great individuals get better because of the adversity.
- You are never defined by a moment. You are defined by an entire body of work.[7]

Now, let's talk about creating a culture for a credible organization. It is important to adhere to certain norms and principles. Here are some suggestions:

- Listen and allow people to express ideas and views.
- Speak honestly and speak privately when necessary.
- Respect each other's commitments as well as your own.
- Be there for each other.
- Acknowledge and appreciate the contributions of the members of your organization.

Culture has some ground rules based on the principles identifying who you are as an organization. How you communicate these principles to all members, regardless of their position in the organization, and how you demonstrate those principles and values will define your culture. Culture has the power to shape our identity. Over time and under the right circumstance, guidance, and modeling, the norms and values of the group to which we belong become our own, so we do not have to think about how we behave any longer. It becomes part of our life.

---

7 Marci Narum, "The Secret Sauce for Any Champion," *Inspired Woman Magazine,* March 28, 2018. https://inspiredwomanonline.com/secret-sauce-champion/

The key to creating and influencing the culture of your organization begins with your leadership. If a leader is not going to practice or model what your organization is all about, it will be translated as lip service or glittery words written on your website or billboards. How can a leader influence the culture of an organization? Communication, communication, communication. It takes relentless communication. Your influence derives from what you say and how you say it. It may also be how often you say it. Whether you are a CEO, team leader, or a manager, you have the power to change a culture by your words and actions.

As I watched the network news about what was going on nationally in our political scene with our central administration in mid-2018, I made some observations. I was reluctant to comment, but the events provide a fascinating case study for examining the culture of the White House administration during that time. I challenge you to consider this subject without getting wrapped up in a particular political affiliation. In a one-year period, many employees left the White House through resignation, termination, investigation, or other reasons. The turnover of employees within this administration was twice what it was during President Bush's first year and triple that of President Obama's first year in office. I will not enter into political discussion, but instead paint a picture about the culture of what was happening in this administration. We saw a 50 percent turnover in the tier one positions. Most of the departing staff, if not all, were supporters of President Trump. Then-President Trump's leadership style induced a culture of unpredictability, or some may call it chaos, within the White House administration. Often, he would speak his mind regarding major policy issues without consulting senior staff, cabinet members, or policy advisors. Occasionally, he criticized his cabinet members in public and expected them to follow his lead. He expected blind loyalty from his staff, which I believe he considered one of his guiding principles. He often communicated based on impulse, sometimes several times a day, by tweeting to the public. He also blindsided some of his own staff about major policy issues. As I mentioned earlier, he often demanded loyalty and support from his senior staff. There was thus a culture of fear within the White House staff. Nevertheless, there were staff members who were supportive and loyal to the president and who appreciated his leadership style.

Another way to affect your organization's culture is to assess its pulse, which can be accomplished by being visible and present whenever possible and connecting with employees at all levels. Reinforce and empower employees appropriately rather than giving throw-away compliments or meaningless rewards. Some companies and organizations reward people without any goals established or any teamwork motives. This approach reminds me of a wonderful story that Ken Blanchard, author of *One Minute Manager*, told at a seminar I attended. He talked about a company that used to give turkeys as gifts to employees on a certain holiday. When the tradition started, employees appreciated the generous gesture from the management. Years later, for many employees, the tradition became an expectation. Since management was not seeing any value in this tradition, however, without warning they decided to stop handing out the turkeys. You can almost predict what happened at this company. People were upset, and many of them questioned, "Where is MY turkey?" Reward people appropriately.

It is important that you take care of the people within your organization so they can, in turn, take care of the customers. Give employees expectations, responsibility, and reinforcement. Culture has a powerful influence in an organization. It affects practically everything from employee expectations to what decisions are made, how employees dress, rituals, and traditions. What is it that determines the kind of culture an organization will have? How will that culture work in the day-to-day life of an organization? Every organization needs good role models who can display and practice the cultural values of the organization. The business environment in which the company operates determines what it must do to be successful. Sometimes rituals and traditions established for the organization are a great way to build cohesive teams, provided they have some direct tie-in with the organizational values rather than being token rituals. Effective communication is the key factor in achieving good results.

A large number of organizations have their beliefs and values proclaimed through websites or other materials that declare their mission and vision. Some organizations even advertise slogans on billboards and other media outlets. Many such organizations are spending marketing dollars to project a positive image. We all make our own value assessment about some of these advertisements based on the message they are communicating to the public.

A few years ago, my wife saw a TV advertisement for a fast-food franchise projecting inappropriate sexual images to entice customers to buy their products. I use the word inappropriate based on our values and judgment. In fact, my wife was very offended by this advertisement, and she instantly changed the channel. She even made a comment to me that she would never buy their products again. Again, we all make value judgments like this based on the image an organization is projecting. The leadership or management usually sets the tone for the organization. In this case, it must have been acceptable to the management to project this image, and it is likely that they may have even done a market study before spending their marketing dollars for this advertisement. In other words, what is acceptable and enticing for one group of people may not be the same for another. There is a correlation between the values that you are upholding and the image or the culture of the organization that you are projecting.

If the management is not leading the organization consistently with the projected values and mission, it is likely that the credibility of the organization will be short-lived. If the employees of an organization comply with the directions provided by the leadership without an opportunity for explanation, discussion, or feedback, it says something about the culture of that organization. Sometimes people comply because they agree with what they are doing, or they may have nothing to contribute for the betterment of the organization. People also comply with the management based on fear of speaking up or losing their job. Some of the employees might be in an 80/20 predicament, not knowing what to do because of the fear of jeopardizing their job security or continuing with an organization that makes them miserable.

Values are the foundation for creating any type of culture in an organization. Values provide a sense of shared direction, define success, and establish standards of achievement. When determining values for the organization, it is essential to identify values that bring employees together and influence the successful operation of an organization. For these values to be effective, they must be shared values defining what the outside world can expect from the organization as well as the expectations of the people whom they serve.

Once the members of the organization understand and agree upon the values and cultural standards, members must understand there is accountability placed at all levels of the organization. Accountability impacts the whole team and helps in accomplishing the organization's goals. When coming up with accountability principles, there must be components such as communication, role modeling, trusting relationships, and avenues for providing feedback — even if there is disagreement — embedded in each component. The consequence for accountability issues should also be a part of this discussion and expectation. Adherence to these principles creates a safe environment.

Here are some suggestions for creating a positive culture for your organization:

- Strong, trusting, encouraging, and respectful relationships between the management and the team are imperative.

- Management must practice servant leadership rather than projecting the image of a boss and subordinates.

- Management and team members must be seen as partners in their mission and must adhere to principles of accountability and transparency.

- Catching people doing something right should be the norm, rather than gotcha tactics.

- The vision and the mission must be the central focus and the driving force.

- Effective communication should be the norm, at the same time adhering to the principles of confidentiality when necessary and appropriate. All members of the team should have a good understanding of the parameters for confidentiality.

The culture of an organization might be described as a family, factory, jungle, or a cathedral or temple. How do you describe your organization? Is it a family where people care about and trust one another? Is your organization a factory where high standards, expectations, and production are the priority? Maybe your organization can be described as a jungle where resources might be scarce, special interests might compete against each other, and territorial conflicts occur. Or is your organization like a cathedral or temple, where people feel they are making a difference and there is a purpose? There are challenges associated with each of these scenarios, and potentially every organization has every one of these scenarios. Be purposeful in creating and sustaining the culture you want to build.

7

TO MANAGE
THE ORGANIZATIONAL
CHANGE PROCESS

Once there was a daughter who was observing her mother getting ready to put a roast in the oven. She noticed her mother was cutting both ends of the roast prior to putting it in the pan for baking, so she asked her mother why she was doing that. The daughter had seen her mother do this many times. Her mother was puzzled and replied, "I don't know, but I saw my mother doing this when I was growing up, so I will ask your grandma the next time I see her." The grandmother later explained simply that she did not have a pan to fit the roast, so she had to cut the edges to make the roasts fit.

Sometimes we do things in a very specific way for a very long time but cannot explain why. Sometimes the action is an entrenched tradition that we cherish, offering only one explanation: we have always done it this way. You may experience the same scenario in your organization. Some people will be protective of traditions or habits even when there are new and progressive ideas proposed. At this juncture, some of the experienced people in the organization may respond, "We tried that before, and it is not going to work."

Change is a threatening concept for most people, and they will resist. Some people may say that they embrace change, but it is usually when the change is not impacting them directly. We are creatures of habit, and we are programmed and patterned individuals. Our perceptions and expectations often influence our thinking and behavior. We are also influenced by our surroundings, and are the products of our previous experiences.

Since I set the stage for some possible challenges when implementing changes in an organization, let's broaden our thinking for a better understanding. A good principle for you to keep in mind is that people usually resist changes that are forced upon them. At the same time, they support changes that they are part of or in which they have a vested interest.

Change affects people differently. Changing behavior is not an instantaneous act. Rather, it is a process that occurs over time and consists of a series of actions. The entire process usually occurs in five different phases: awareness, interest, evaluation, trial, and adoption.[8] Before an individual can adopt a new practice or concept, a person must first develop an interest in the idea to the extent that the person seeks further information about it. The individual will then mentally evaluate the concept. If the concept seems to be a good idea, the person may then give it a try. If the results are favorable, people may adopt the idea. The rate of adoption of new ideas varies greatly from person to person. Some individuals are quick to adopt, while others are very slow or may never adopt a particular idea.

Differing adoption rates have led researchers to define five categories of adopters: Innovators, Early Adopters, Early Majority, Late Majority, and Laggards.[9] These are categorical descriptions of human behavior, not value judgments as to whether adoption of the idea is inherently good or bad. We are often influenced by our surroundings. Sometimes our perceptions and expectations shape our thinking and behavior. We respond to those things that are important to us. Individuals need sufficient time and information to work their way through the adoption process for themselves.

Because we are creatures of habit, the introduction of something new contains the potential of threat as well as progress. When we talk about doing something differently, we are talking about change. As we approach crossroads and consider new program directions, we must also consider how people cope with change. There are two categories of change. One type is unplanned, which will create a reactive change process for others because they were not part of creating the idea. The other type is planned, a proactive process where others are a part of creating the idea.

---

[8] See Everett M. Rogers, *Diffusion of Innovations* (New York: The Free Press, a division of Simon & Schuster, 1962).
[9] *Ibid.*

Some people experience the change process similarly to the grieving process through denial, anger, acceptance, change, and energy.[10]

If a new CEO, president, or an administrator decides to initiate some changes in the organization that you are serving, it would be great for the leader who is launching the change to understand the short- and long-term impacts of change.

We also must recognize that people are faced with different levels of change. We adopt changes differently based on the following factors: knowledge, skills, attitude, and values.[11] I will walk through these areas one by one. The Organizational Change Factors chart explains the difficulty in terms of dealing with these factors when change is initiated in an organization.[12]

If implemented changes in an organization have an impact on you, and if the changes are impacting people at the knowledge level, you can do something about it. You can educate the employees about the changes being initiated and explain the rationale. If you involve people early in this process, you can teach them and instill ownership and confidence in the process. If the change process has an impact on people at the knowledge level, correction is comparatively easy through education and participation.

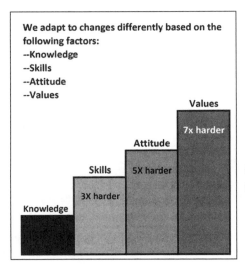

Organizational Change Factors

---

10 Elizabeth Kübler-Ross and David Kessler, *On Grief and Grieving: Finding the Meaning of Grief Through the Five Stages of Loss* (Simon & Schuster, 2005).
11 Mohan Kumar, "The relationship between beliefs, values, attitudes and behaviors," *Owlcation Social Sciences Psychology*. https://owlcation.com/social-sciences/Teaching-and-Assessing-Attitudes.
12 See Edwin H. Amend, *Change!! Who, Me?* (Fargo: NDSU Cooperative Extension Service, 1985).

If the change process is having an impact at the skills level, it will be three times harder for employees to buy-in or adopt the change than at the knowledge level. I distinctly remember in the early '80s when a new computer system was implemented throughout the North Dakota University System without much consultation or warning; people panicked and resisted. Several employees who were within five years of retirement took the option to retire early rather than deal with this significant change that challenged them at the knowledge and skills levels. Some people did not have that option or could not afford to retire, so they had to learn the new system. In this situation, learning new skills became a necessary step to move forward. Most people will calculate the risks and consequences of not adopting changes and come on board.

As you can see, implementing change is already getting harder, and if the changes you are making is having an impact at the attitudinal level, it will be five times harder than at the knowledge level. In every organization, you are going to find people resisting change even before they learn about what the changes are and how it is going to impact them. Some of them have preconceived notions about the change or simply have a negative attitude about any type of change. Sometimes these people also influence others in the organization and impact them negatively. So, it is important for the person initiating the change to calculate these factors and be proactive about the change process by involving and educating the entire team from the start.

The final stage or factor is the hardest one to deal with. It is seven times harder to change values than it is to change knowledge. As we discussed extensively about values earlier, there may not be a compromise about certain values. This scenario presents another situation where the 80/20 Principle comes into play. Divisive national issues such as gun control, abortion, affordable care, or immigration are but a few examples where people might experience an impact at the values level. People on both sides of the debates will dig in their heels, unwilling to compromise.

Some people may experience more than one of the four change factors, so you must be prepared with a strategy to move forward with a plan of action by always involving and educating people in the change process, preferably from the initial knowledge stage.

Two more factors to consider are individual and group behavior. I am sure it is no surprise that changing group behavior is a much harder task than changing individual behavior. The effort is also very time consuming,

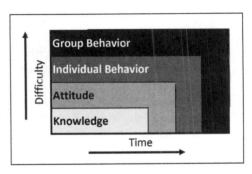

Group vs.
Individual Change

so be proactive and be prepared as you get ready to initiate a new plan for your organization.

As outlined by Ken Hultman in *Managing Resistance to Change*, we see that when the change process is initiated, people's reactions might fall into one of the following categories.[13]

1. *Acceptance.* People who accept the change are often cooperative, enthusiastic, and in some cases passive.

2. *Indifference.* People who are indifferent to the changes are often apathetic and will do only what is required of them.

3. *Passive resistance.* The people who fit into this category will do as little as possible, just to keep their job. You may also find some of these resisters collaborating with other members of the team by negatively influencing them by showing their disagreement.

4. *Active resistance.* This group of people might try to sabotage the organization through inappropriate and unacceptable behavior. They may also be purposeful in committing errors to show negative results.

People usually resist change when:
- The purpose is ambiguous or general.
- They have inadequate information.
- They are not involved in change which affects them.
- The request is based solely on a personal appeal.
- There is lack of trust in the change initiated.
- Work group norms are ignored.
- They are satisfied with the status quo, so they see no need for change.
- Rewards for making changes are inadequate.
- Change is simply for the sake of change or made too rapidly.
- It creates excessive work pressure.

---

13 Ken E. Hultman, "Managing resistance to change," in *Encyclopedia of Information Systems*, vol. 3 (San Diego, CA: Academic Press, 2014), pp. 693–704.

People are more likely to positively respond to leadership when:
- The change is specific.
- They have sufficient information.
- They are involved in bringing about change which affects them.
- They understand how the change will affect them and how they may benefit from it.
- Present norms are taken into account.
- They perceive a need for change and feel that they will be adequately rewarded for making the change.
- Timing of the change is appropriate.
- Change can be accommodated without undue work pressure.

You will likely encounter some challenges as you initiate changes in an organization, Be prepared for people to resist change just because they don't like any type of change. There will be people declaring, "If it isn't broken, don't fix it." Others will resist simply because they have always done it a certain way. The second major challenge you may encounter might be regarding your financial or human resources. Are there new expenses? Where is the money going to come from for these additional costs? Maybe your organization is already spread too thinly in terms of staffing. Another challenge for which you may need to be prepared is public perception and their understanding, particularly if your organization is supported at least partially by public funds.

You may also experience some challenges within the organization if you are making some structural changes and not following the appropriate process. Let me provide a scenario to explain this further. Sometimes organizations reorganize and create structure to benefit certain people rather than basing change on good rationale to meet the mission, vision, and goals of the organization. If you are making organizational changes strictly to benefit a certain person by creating a job description to fit into this person's qualifications, this is an example of beating the system to avoid public criticism and scrutiny.

How can you be a change agent in making positive changes in your organization? It begins with you and your attitude. You need to be deliberate about your attitude as well as adhering to good processes and principles of change so that you will gain as much or more than the organization. As a change agent, you need to take ownership of the changes rather than simply acting as a spectator. You also need to choose your battles carefully and be tolerant of the organization's mistakes. I am not suggesting you sacrifice your values and principles. Be purposeful.

8

WE ARE CALLED TO LEADERSHIP

...

TO BE A SERVANT

Are you a servant leader? My father was the best servant leader I have ever known in my life, so I decided to dedicate this chapter in his honor. I am sure most of you are familiar with the servant leadership model, where service is the foundation. Serving others is the primary goal. Servant leaders put others first in hopes of creating a sense of community. You become part of this community through giving. There is a wonderful quote from the Dalai Lama that goes something like this: "If you seek enlightenment for yourself to enable you to serve others, you are with purpose."

In what turned out to be one of his last speeches, Martin Luther King said, "Everybody can be great because anybody can serve." Serving others can be accomplished in many ways. When we are dedicated to identifying and meeting the needs of others, we will often be put into the position of having to make sacrifices. When we serve others, sometimes we will have to forgive and give others credit even if we do not feel like it because it is the right thing to do.

As I mentioned earlier, my father was a servant leader. He was a Christian pastor who had the great fortune to attend several prayer meetings with Mahatma Gandhi during the Indian Independence Movement. I remember my father describing these prayer meetings as interfaith gatherings.

Let me narrate a story that made an impact on me but may not have any relevance to the topic at hand, other than both Gandhi and my father were servant leaders. During the Independence Movement, Gandhi conducted prayer meetings every morning, and leaders from various religions took turns assisting. My father was one of the very few Christians to attend these prayer meetings. When it was the Christians' turn, Gandhi often requested the hymn "Abide with Me." India became independent in 1947, and since then, when the people celebrate Independence and Republic Day, it is customary for the military band to play Gandhi's favorite hymn. Until I saw a YouTube video of the hymn played at a Republic Day ceremony in India, I thought the story was just one of many my father told us when we were growing up. To this day, when I see the band playing the hymn, I get goosebumps because I recognize the influence my father may have had in Gandhi's life and vice versa.

Each of us has the capacity to make a difference in another person's life. Great leaders from the past like Gandhi, Mother Teresa, Martin Luther King, and Nelson Mandela often found great joy in serving others. What they had in common was their passion to serve others, which was demonstrated in their life through their actions. In fact, they practiced servant leadership. The good news is that anyone can serve others. The key to servant leadership is giving priority to others before promoting oneself. In my opinion, this is a value.

So, what is servant leadership and who is a servant leader? Here are some fundamental characteristics.

- Servant leaders serve others first. If you are the type of person needing to be the center of attention, you may not be a good candidate to be a servant leader.
- Servant leadership is a transformational approach to both life and work. There has to be a transformation taking place in your life, rather than simply proclaiming that you are a servant leader.
- Servant leaders are stewards, and they are accountable for the well-being of the larger community. Some people think servant leadership is only for warm, fuzzy people with passive leadership styles. Up until about three to four decades ago, being a servant leader was not popular.
- Servant leadership is all about doing the right thing for the right reason and standing up for what is right.

Where did this model come from? From my readings over the years on the topic of servant leadership, I find a consensus that the model began with Jesus, the first person who taught the concept of servant leadership. Jesus took the approach of a servant leader and clearly identified his purpose for his followers and gave them direction. Jesus said in Matthew 20:26, "Whoever wishes to become great among you shall be your servant."

I grew up in India, and as a child I learned the negative connotation of the word servant. We always had servants in our home even though our parents considered them as part of our family. Some people will say that the words servant and leader do not go together. Based on my cultural orientation, I can understand why it might be difficult to conceptualize and act both as a leader and servant who leads. But things have changed. In my life, there was no disconnect because of how my father and mother modeled servant leadership for me as well as in the community at large. For others, it has become popular to identify as a servant leader because several world leaders have embraced themselves as servant leaders. I am not sure if they all practice it, but many of them claim themselves to be servant leaders.

The key to servant leadership is giving priority to others. If we start promoting ourselves, our ego will dictate our leadership. The Bible says whoever wants to be a leader among you must be a servant and whoever wants to be first among you must become a slave. Jesus got down on his hands and knees and washed the feet of his disciples. This is what humility is all about. Humility is an important ingredient of servant leadership.[14]

Promoting yourself should be absent from the list. I had a principle that I often shared with my staff that it was not their job to make themselves look good; instead, it was our job to make the people whom we served look good. This included my supervisor and the people whom I served.

If you truly would like to practice servant leadership, you need to make a personal commitment to being an effective leader who is willing to model servanthood in your personal and professional life. These are some steps that you need to take in this process. First, you need to know who and what you are as a person. This understanding will identify your values and principles about how you live your life as well as help you to put them into practice. Second, you need to keep your ego under check, because humility is a critical component of this leadership. You must be willing to receive feedback, even when it may reveal some painful truth about you. Third, you must decide if you are willing to make the necessary commitment. As I mentioned in the definition, becoming a servant leader is a transformative and life-changing process.

---

14 See Ken Blanchard and Phil Hodges, *Lead like Jesus* (Nashville: Thomas Nelson, 2008).

How do you develop servant leaders in the community? John W. Gardner, former Secretary of US Department of Health, Education, and Welfare, provided four principles that are necessary for you to become a leader as well as a model citizen of your community and the global society. I do not believe Secretary Gardner wrote these principles as a template for servant leadership, but they fit well with the servant leadership model.[15]

1. **Releasing human potential:** What does this mean? It is important for you to know your strengths and your potential so you can utilize them or unleash them in a positive way. In other words, you cannot give until you know who you are as a person.

2. **Balancing the needs of the individual and the community:** Leadership must benefit not only our own personal and professional needs, but it also must satisfy the needs of the community. How often have you heard about people getting involved in leadership roles simply to benefit their personal needs or to strengthen their resume? If you are doing this only for your personal gain, you are violating the basic principles involved in being a servant leader. Servant leadership has to be a high priority in your leadership commitment. What you gain through your leadership has to be balanced with what you contribute to the community. Identify your own values first and then understand the values of the community or the organization so that your values and the community values are compatible.

3. **Defending the fundamental values of the community:** In order for you to defend the values of the community you seek to serve, you need to become involved and learn about the values, needs, and wants that give the community its unique personality. This includes understanding how decisions are made and the process. Here again, if you know your own values as well as the culture, values, needs, and wants of the community, your service to the community will have more of an impact.

4. **Having a sense of initiative and responsibility:** Sometimes we get involved in an organization simply to be a part of that group. I believe that responsibility and initiative come from commitment. Commitment is a loaded word. A leader must make the commitment and take the initiative to be responsible.

[15] John Gardner, *On Leadership* (New York: Simon & Schuster, 1993).

If you practice these principles, you will become a model citizen of the community and the global society.

Let me use a metaphor of two seas in Palestine to provide some good insight about serving others in your life. The river Jordan flows into the Sea of Galilee with sparkling water from the hills. People build homes near it. This sea is fresh, fish live in it, and bushes and trees grow near it. The same river Jordan also flows south into another sea, the Dead Sea. There are no fish or greenery, and the air is stale.[16]

What makes the difference between these neighboring seas? The Jordan River empties the same good water into the Sea of Galilee and the Dead Sea. The difference is that the Sea of Galilee receives water but does not keep it. For every drop that flows in, another drop flows out. The giving and receiving goes on in equal measure. The other sea gives nothing and flows nowhere; that is why it is called the Dead Sea.

There are also two kinds of people in this world. There are people who receive without giving back and then there are the givers. The question is, are we behaving like the Sea of Galilee by giving and receiving in equal measures, or are we like the Dead Sea? You can become part of a community through giving. When more and more people model this in a community, your community will become richer in the spirit of serving.

Servant leadership is also a living statement of how we treat one another and how we demonstrate unconditional love. I learned this through my Christian faith, and maybe you learned through another faith. Jesus took the approach of a servant leader and influenced the lives of people and empowered them to change the world with a clearly identified purpose.

The River Jordan as a Metaphor for Servant Leadership

---

[16] See Glenn Van Ekeren, *Speaker's Sourcebook II: Quotes, Stories, and Anecdotes for Every Occasion* (New York: Penguin Putnam, Inc., 1994).

An important aspect of servant leadership is not just what we accomplish, but what we have left behind. The student government at NDSU where I worked for many years has a motto, which is to leave the place better than you found it. They seem to understand what true servant leadership is about.

Jesus gave us the charge to serve rather than be served even when we are faced with challenges in our lives. Servant leaders will always be looking at the possibility of serving others for the common good. Self-serving leaders will spend very little time in the best interests of others.

As I mentioned earlier, the primary principle behind servant leadership is to serve others first. According to James C. Hunter, author of *The World's Most Powerful Leadership Principle*, a servant leader should have the skill of influencing people to work enthusiastically toward goals identified as being for the common good and to carry character that inspires confidence.

Leadership is a process of influencing and developing others to accomplish a shared goal. Leaders are making a personal choice about how and to what end they will use their influence. If your actions are driven by service and dedication to a cause or relationship, then you will model and encourage these values in others. Are you a servant leader wherever you go?

According to Jim Collins, author of *Good to Great*,

> **when things are going well for self-serving leaders, they look in the mirror, beat their chests, and tell themselves how good they are. When things go wrong, they look out the window and blame everyone else. Great leaders on the other hand, are humble. When things go well, they look out the window and give everyone else credit. When things go wrong, these servant leaders look in the mirror and ask, "what could I have done differently to allow these people to be as great as they could be?" Servant leaders have solid self-esteem. As a result, they are willing to admit when they have a weakness or need assistance. Servant leaders also receive feedback freely.[17]**

One of the problems we see in the lives of leaders today is that they love to tell everyone else how they should serve and act, yet when it comes to their own lives, they do not practice what they are preaching. Too often there is a real disconnect between what the leader says and what a leader does.

---

[17] See Jim Collins, *Good to Great: Why Some Companies Make the Leap and Others Don't* (New York: HarperCollins, 2001).

Our human tendency, according to Matthew 7:3, is to see the speck in our brother's eye and not to notice the log in our own eye. So do not make the mistake of trying to change others without focusing on yourself first. As Gandhi would say, "Be the change you want to see in others."

Leaders often define success based on power, position, performance, and opinions of others. Personally, in my life, my success is based on my relationship with my God and the choices that I have made and will continue to make in my life every day. Leadership is not about your position, title, or the amount of money you make; it is all about how you serve others. It is not simply talking about it but doing it.

According to Blanchard and Hodges, one of the basic foundations of servant leadership is trust. Trust is the glue that holds relationships together. A manager or leader who does not believe or trust their employees to do a good job is not a good candidate for servant leadership.

There is no blind loyalty in servant leadership. As I stated several times earlier, a servant does not operate out of ego and does not expect the loyalty to the boss (a term you would not use in servant leadership); instead, the servant leader understands the true nature of loyalty, which is a nurturing relationship. Loyalty should work both ways and should not be influenced by power. Loyalty to employees means being honest and trusting, treating people with respect, responding appropriately, and acting with integrity.

Serving others can be accomplished in many ways. People and organizations work more effectively if a clear vision and values are established up front. Servant leaders always model their values in the way they treat other people.

Values are the guiding principles that define character in a leader. We all know that understanding who you are as a person helps you identify your beliefs and values. Remember, values are the glue that holds life's demanding details in place. How do you want to be remembered when you leave this world? It is about leaving a leadership legacy of service. What do you stand for? What are your guiding principles? Values are the non-negotiable principles that define character in a leader. As Rick Warren, author of *The Purpose Driven Life*, reminds us, our character is essentially the sum of our habits.

Value Choices: 80/20

Many organizations have established and declared their organizational values publicly. At the same time, many of the employees are not aligned with their organization's values. Conflicts between organizational values and personal values are a reality of life. What do you do when the values of the organizations do not align with your own values? You may realize this over time as you experience ongoing gaps between established purpose and values and what is acted out on a day-to-day basis. At this point, you are faced with a choice of compromising your values, being a change agent in the organization, or leaving.

We make choices about values in our lives all the time. Life and leadership are all about choices. Choices are made based on your values whether you admit it or not. In an organization, if a leader does not respond to the needs and desires of employees, those people will not take good care of their customers.

Again, Jesus modeled the ultimate servant leadership by giving clear directions to his disciples and holding them accountable. In tough situations, people will look to the leaders to see how they respond. This will be a true test to see if they will stay on course and remain true to their mission and values. I could not agree more strongly with Ken Blanchard that servant leadership starts with a vision and ends with a servant heart that helps people act and live according to that vision.

Finally, I ask that you consider the following Bible verse:

What does the Lord require of you but to do justice, and to love kindness, and to walk humbly with your God? (Micah 6:8)

We are called to be servant leaders, and by doing this we help our organizations to do what is good and to act justly through service.

CONTRIBUTORS

Diana M. Doyle has been president of Arapahoe Community College since April 2010 and has more than forty-one years of progressive professional experience in higher education. Prior to joining ACC, Doyle was the executive vice president of Learning & Student Affairs at the Community College of Denver and twice served as interim president at Western Nebraska Community College where she was the vice president of Instruction & Student Services. Dr. Doyle's professional career also includes leadership roles at Colorado School of Mines, University of Nebraska-Lincoln, and Illinois State University.

She was president of the national professional association NASPA—Student Affairs Administrators in Higher Education in 2008 to 2009. In addition, she was the recipient of numerous awards and recognition including the 2018 NASPA Region 4West Presidential Excellence Award, the national community college honorary society Phi Theta Kappa Shirley B. Gordon Presidential Award of Distinction in 2016, and the 2014 President of the Year Award from the State Student Advisory Council in Colorado. In 2010, she received the NASPA Foundation Pillar of the Profession award for outstanding contributions to college student success. Doyle earned her PhD in Public Administration from the University of Colorado-Denver and holds bachelor and master's degrees from Illinois State University.

Gwendolyn Jordan Dungy served as executive director emeritus of NASPA, a professional association for student affairs administrators. Since retirement from NASPA in 2012, she has served as senior vice president for Student Services at Montgomery College in Maryland, a community college educating sixty thousand students on three main campuses. She is actively engaged in executive coaching, consulting on diversity, inclusion, and equity, and writing. Among her publications is a blog titled, "It's About Students." She recently contributed an article to the fiftieth anniversary issue of *Change: The Magazine of Higher Education*.

Eric Grospitch serves as the vice president for Student Life at Washburn University where he works with Counseling & Health Services, Student Recreation and Wellness, Residential Living, University Diversity & Inclusion, Student Activities & Greek Life, Veteran Services, and Career Services. Previously he was the assistant vice chancellor and dean of students at the

University of Missouri Kansas City. He has led a number of strategic planning initiatives including the implementation of long-term maintenance budgeting, fraternity and sorority planning, a student customer service training program, campus safety, diversity education, and transportation initiatives. Eric received his bachelor's degree in business and master's in counseling from Fort Hays State University and his EdD in educational policy and leadership from the University of Kansas.

Kate Haugen received an undergraduate degree from Luther College in Decorah, Iowa, and master's and PhD degrees from the University of Iowa. She held numerous positions in her forty-two-year professional career in student affairs, alumni relations, and development in higher education at Luther College, the University of Iowa, the University of Minnesota, and North Dakota State University. Before her retirement in 2013, she served as associate vice president for Student Affairs at North Dakota State University.

Bruce Maylath is a professor of English at North Dakota State University, where he directs the university's program in Upper-Division Writing and where he teaches courses in linguistics and international technical writing. He is the author of many articles and the co-editor of eight books, the most recent of which is *Translation & Localization* (Routledge, 2019). He is an elder of First Presbyterian Church of Fargo, where he leads a Bible study for men.

Laura Oster-Aaland serves as vice provost for Student Affairs and Enrollment Management at North Dakota State University where she oversees the offices of Admission, Counseling, Financial Aid and Scholarships, Enrollment Management Administrative Systems, One Stop, Student Conduct, Student Activities, Student Health Service, and Student Success Programs. Over her nearly thirty-year career at NDSU, previous positions held by Oster-Aaland include associate vice provost for Enrollment Management, dean of Enrollment Management, director of Student Success Programs, lecturer in Communication, and director of Annual Giving.

George Wallman earned his undergraduate degree from Luther College in Decorah, Iowa, a master's degree from Northern Illinois University, and his PhD degree from Michigan State University. He served as director of Admissions at Luther College and retired from North Dakota State University after serving as vice president of Student Affairs for more than fifteen years. His insights into organizational process began while taking a class at Michigan State University from Gene Jennings in the College of Business and were further developed as he served in administrative positions at Luther College, NDSU, and as a consultant-evaluator for the Higher Learning Commission.

REFERENCES

Amend, Edwin H. *Change!! Who, Me?* Fargo: NDSU Cooperative Extension Service, 1985.

Anderson, Dave. *Up Your Business!: 7 Steps to Fix, Build, Or Stretch Your Organization.* Hoboken: John Wiley & Sons, 2010.

Berghofer, Desmond. Institute for ethical leadership. Doing the right thing. http://www.ethicalleadership.com/DoingRightThing.htm

Blanchard, Ken, Patricia Zigarmi, and Drea Zigarmi. *Leadership and the One Minute Manager: Increasing Effectiveness Through Situational Leadership.* London: Fontana, 1985.

Blanchard, Ken and Phil Hodges. *Lead like Jesus.* Nashville: Thomas Nelson, 2008.

Blanchard, Kenneth and Norman Vincent Peale. *The Power of Ethical Management.* New York: Random House, 2011.

Brooks, David. *The Road to Character.* New York: Random House, 2015.

Burns, James M. *Leadership.* New York: Harper & Row, 1978.

Collins, Jim. *Good to Great: Why Some Companies Make the Leap and Others Don't.* New York: HarperCollins, 2001.

Covey, Stephen R. *Principle-Centered Leadership.* Simon & Schuster, 1992.

Duckworth, Angela. *Grit: The Power of Passion and Perseverance.* New York: Scribner, 2016.

Gardner, John W. *On Leadership.* New York: Simon & Schuster, 1993.

Gladwell, Malcolm. *Blink: The Power of Thinking Without Thinking.* CNIB, 2012.

Grant, A. "Power doesn't corrupt. It just exposes who leaders really are." February 22, 2019. https://www.washingtonpost.com/business/economy/power-doesnt-corrupt-it-just-exposes-who-leaders-really-are/2019/02/22/f5680116-3600-11e9-854a-7a14d7fec96a_story.html?noredirect=on&utm_term=.1552f36be1fd

Greenleaf, Robert K. *Servant Leadership: A Journey into the Nature of Legitimate Power and Greatness.* Mahwah: Paulist Press, 1979.

Frick, Don M. and Larry C. Spears, eds. *On Becoming a Servant Leader: The Private Writings of Robert K. Greenleaf.* San Francisco: Jossey-Bass, 1996.

Hultman, Ken E. "Managing resistance to change." *Encyclopedia of Information Systems,* Volume 3. San Diego, CA, 2003.

Hunter, C. J. *The world's most powerful leadership principle: How to become a servant leader.* Crown Business, 2004.

Jennings, E. E. *Routes to the Executive Suite,* 1971.

Kilgour, D.M. and C. Eden. Introduction to the handbook of group decision and negotiation. *In Handbook of group decision and negotiation* (pp. 1–7). Springer, Dordrecht, 2010..

Kouzes, James M., and Barry Z. Posner. *Credibility: How Leaders Gain and Lose It, Why People Demand It,* 2nd ed. San Francisco: John Wiley & Sons, 2011.

Kübler-Ross, Elizabeth and David Kessler. *On Grief and Grieving: Finding the Meaning of Grief Through the Five Stages of Loss.* Simon and Schuster, 2005.

Kumar, Mohan. *The relationship between beliefs, values, attitudes and behaviors.* Owlcation Social Sciences Psychology, 2018. https://owlcation.com/social-sciences/Teaching-and-Assessing-Attitudes

Maxwell, John C. *The 21 Irrefutable Laws of Leadership: Follow Them and People Will Follow You.* Nashville: Thomas Nelson, 2007.

Narum, M. "The secret sauce for any champion." *Inspired Woman Magazine,* March 28, 2018. https://inspiredwomanonline.com/secret-sauce-champion/

Palmer, Parker J. *Let Your Life Speak: Listening for the Voice of Vocation.* San Francisco: John Wiley & Sons, 1999.

Peale, Norman V. *The Power of Positive Thinking; The Positive Principle Today; Enthusiasm Makes the Differences.* Wings Books, 1952.

Rogers, Everett M. *Diffusion of Innovations.* New York: The Free Press, a division of Simon & Schuster, 1962.

Shank, Gary D. *Qualitative Research: A Personal Skills Approach.* Pearson Merrill Prentice Hall, 2006.

Van Ekeren, Glenn. *Speaker's Sourcebook II: Quotes, Stories, and Anecdotes for Every Occasion.* New York: Penguin Putnam, Inc, 1994.

Warren, Rick. *The Purpose Driven Life: What on Earth Am I Here For?* Zondervan, 2012.

INDEX

*Page numbers in **bold** type indicate photographs or charts.*

ABOUT THE AUTHOR

Prakash Mathew came to Fargo, North Dakota, in 1971 from India after receiving his bachelor's degree in Agriculture and Rural Sociology from Allahabad Agricultural Institute. He earned his master's degree in Counseling and Guidance from North Dakota State University. Prakash held positions at NDSU and Mankato State University including Hall Director, Director of Residence Life, Associate Dean, Dean of Student Life, and Vice President for Student Affairs.

Prakash retired after thirty-eight years of service in student affairs. He currently serves as Vice President Emeritus. Following his retirement in 2014, Prakash served as the Interim Director of Athletics at NDSU.

Prakash provided leadership at the state, regional, and national levels while working in student affairs. He served the National Association of Student Affairs Administrators as a member of the NASPA Foundation, the National Board of Directors, and as regional Vice President. He also served on the Executive Committee for the Council of Student Affairs for the Association of Public and Land-grant Universities.

Prakash continues to provide leadership at the local and regional level serving as a board member of several prominent organizations and a presenter on various leadership models. He has received numerous awards including the NASPA Pillar of the Profession, the NASPA Region IV West Distinguished Service Award, the James J. Rhatigan Outstanding Dean Award, Blue Key Doctor of Service Award, and the NASPA Scott Goodnight Award for Outstanding Performance as Dean.

Prakash and his wife, Jane, lead an active life in the Fargo area, where he enjoys his time outdoors as a master gardener. He is the proud parent of sons Christopher and Trevor and daughter-in-law Emily, and he is the proud grandpa to Isabelle and Zara.

ABOUT THE PRESS

North Dakota State University Press (NDSU Press) exists to stimulate and coordinate interdisciplinary regional scholarship. These regions include the Red River Valley, the state of North Dakota, the plains of North America (comprising both the Great Plains of the United States and the prairies of Canada), and comparable regions of other continents. We publish peer reviewed regional scholarship shaped by national and international events and comparative studies.

Neither topic nor discipline limits the scope of NDSU Press publications. We consider manuscripts in any field of learning. We define our scope, however, by a regional focus in accord with the press's mission. Generally, works published by NDSU Press address regional life directly, as the subject of study. Such works contribute to scholarly knowledge of region (that is, discovery of new knowledge) or to public consciousness of region (that is, dissemination of information, or interpretation of regional experience). Where regions abroad are treated, either for comparison or because of ties to those North American regions of primary concern to the press, the linkages are made plain. For nearly three-quarters of a century, NDSU Press has published substantial trade books, but the line of publications is not limited to that genre. We also publish textbooks (at any level), reference books, anthologies, reprints, papers, proceedings, and monographs. The press also considers works of poetry or fiction, provided they are established regional classics or they promise to assume landmark or reference status for the region. We select biographical or autobiographical works carefully for their prospective contribution to regional knowledge and culture. All publications, in whatever genre, are of such quality and substance as to embellish the imprint of NDSU Press.

We changed our imprint to North Dakota State University Press in January 2016. Prior to that, and since 1950, we published as the North Dakota Institute for Regional Studies Press. We continue to operate under the umbrella of the North Dakota Institute for Regional Studies, located at North Dakota State University.